Thankability

30 Days To A Thankful Heart

Jeff & Michelle Niederstadt

This book is dedicated to our Lord and Savior Jesus Christ, for it is by His grace alone that we are where we are today. Because of you, Lord, we are truly able to give thanks in everything.

Contributing Editors
David Mialaret
Kevin Burke
Lee Castello

Design & Graphics
Amy Brunet

THANKABILITY

Table of Contents

30 Days To A Thankful   *H*eart

    *E*verything

    *A*dversity

    *R*eaping

    e*T*ernity

THANKABILITY

Thank – to express gratitude or appreciation to.

Ability – power or capacity to do or act physically, mentally, legally morally or financially.

Thankability – the power or capacity to express gratitude or appreciation.

As my wife and I were discussing this book, we went round and round about a creative, captivating title. We had plenty of ideas about the book, but didn't feel we could begin writing until we had a title. We knew it needed to be something that would catch people's attention and intrigue them to want to know more. So, we discussed this concept of thankfulness and our ability to live that type of life. We never seemed to hit the nail on the head. We had been driving to Houston with our family for the majority of our discussion – and so decided to ask our oldest daughter what she thought. Without a moment's hesitation she said "How about Thankability?" We both looked at each other and smiled, knowing once again God used a child to speak. Thankability it was!

Just because we have a catchy title for the book doesn't necessarily mean that you will read it. In fact, you probably have a couple of questions that immediately come to mind. The first one is why should I read a book about being thankful? Well I'm glad you asked.

After getting the title down, a general outline and a basic concept (which is to read for six days for five weeks for a total of thirty days), I began to think about the whole idea of being thankful, studying, praying, meditating on God's word you get the picture. And I came across a section of scripture that puzzled me. In Galatians 5 verse 22-23 it says, *"But the fruit of the Spirit is love, joy, peace, patience, kindness, goodness, faithfulness, gentleness and self-control. Against such things there is no law."* (NIV) Now it wasn't what was in the verse that puzzled me for I had known of it long before. But what I was puzzled about was what was missing. For the first time, I noticed that thankfulness was not one of the fruits of the Spirit. I'm sure that this is not a new revelation for some of you, but I never thought about what wasn't on the list before. So when I figured out that thankfulness wasn't part of the list I started to wonder why not? Immediately, I thought of Psalm 100 where it says *"Enter into His gates with thanksgiving, and into His courts with praise. Be thankful to Him, and bless His name."* (NKJV)

I realized that the reason thankfulness wasn't one of the fruits of the Spirit was because it was really an act of worship just like praise.   Think about it.   The fruits of the Spirit are primarily demonstrated in our interaction with others, but thankfulness is primarily directed toward God as worship. Every time that we thank Him for our daily bread or for any gift that He's given us we are entering into His presence through worship. So if we can become closer to God by learning how to become more thankful then sign me up. I want to be in His presence. I want to be with Him and enter into His gates and sit in His courts.

But if that's still not a good enough reason for you to read the book maybe this will help. In 1Timothy 6:6 it says that godliness with contentment (being thankful in your current situation) brings great gain. Now it doesn't say specifically what that great gain is but I can assure you that it isn't anything bad. Gaining good things is a very good thing. In fact, I intend to show you that being thankful can bring you great gain in several different ways, the first being spiritually. Being thankful can reap many benefits for you like peace and joy. Peace and joy are gifts that come from God, and as we are thankful toward Him, He is quick to pour out His supernatural blessings into our lives. Second, emotionally there is great benefit in being thankful instead of being depressed and worried. Some of the emotional benefits are happiness and hope. In fact, this concept was proven in a 1998 Gallup poll that showed more than 90% of Americans believed that expressing gratitude makes them happy (www.drwalt.com). Grateful people are less angry, less negative and usually look for the cup to be half full.

Third, the physical benefits of being thankful include less stress and prospering in body as well as your soul. There have been many studies done that have shown the affects of being thankful and what a difference that it can make in your life. According to a study done by the University of California at Davis, researchers found that practicing gratitude can lower your blood pressure and make you feel less hostile. Studies by Cornell University researchers have shown that those who are thankful appear to have lower risks of developing phobias, alcoholism, even depression. They even have stronger immune systems (www.pagingdrgupta.blogs.cnn.com). Whatever it is you are lacking in your life there is no better way to change that than to thank God for what you already have, no matter how small it may be and watch what God does with it.

If you're still not convinced then know that there is no greater way that you could be a living testimony then to be thankful during difficult times no matter what type of adversity you may be facing. Jesus taught that you are the light of the world, and when you light a candle you don' t hide it under a bushel but put it on a lamp stand for all to see. (Matthew 5:14-16) When you are thankful despite the conditions of the world, you are putting your lamp on a stand as a testimony to others of the hope that God has given you.

People notice when you are grateful and people notice when you are ungrateful. At the restaurant where I work we held a promotion where veterans eat free. There was a menu of six items to choose from and the drink and tip were not included. There was an amazing response and the restaurant was filled with war heroes, soldiers and service men and women who have defended our country. Although it was a great day, there were a few people who complained about the promotion. They said we should have included drinks or we should have had more menu items to choose from or we should have offered the bigger steak. But there was one man at our restaurant amidst the busyness and commotion who asked to see the manager who had a different attitude. Now when someone asks to see the manager it is usually not a good thing and I already had several complaints by this point, but this man was shining his light. He indicated that he and his daughter had eaten and had a wonderful meal. He continued by stating he had only been thanked for his service to our country one other time and he was extremely grateful for what the restaurant had done for him and for veterans. This man was a living testimony of being thankful. Even though things could have been better or different he chose to be thankful for what he had received, and it was a shining light for all to see in comparison to the complaints we had heard.

So arise and shine your light as you read this book and gain a greater ability to be thankful because others will be changed by it as well. Even if you are already thankful, reading this book will encourage you in your thankfulness and allow you to enter into His gates, bring great gain in your life, and provide tangible opportunities for your light to shine.

It is my hope and prayer that through this book, God is glorified and you are more grateful, and have a more accurate perception of God's love for you and the blessings He has given you. It is also my hope that you are more content about what you have, about what you do for a living, and about who you are. I pray that through this book that God will pour out His mercy and grace into your life in miraculous and unexplainable ways. One day while I was spending time with God, He gave me a revelation that He didn't care about what things looked like on the outside of my life. He was pleased with me on the inside and it didn't matter if I was a perfect picture of success with a large home and two Lexus'. He was pleased with me because of my decisions, my integrity and my character, and not what others could see. Ultimately, God is pleased with me because of His Son Jesus and not for anything that I can bring to the table. So it is my hope that after this study you will feel God's pleasure, not for what you've accomplished or for what you have, but for who you are becoming in His Son. God wants you to have all kinds of good things, but even if you don't, God is still pleased with you and wants you to know how proud He is of you and how much He cares about you.

When we're not thankful, we take things for granted. And when we take things for granted we can lose what we have. When we are not thankful for our possessions, we let them rust and decay. When we are not thankful for our freedom, we do not vote. When we are not thankful for life we murder and abort. When we are not thankful for our house, we buy a bigger one we can't afford. When we are not thankful for the covenant of marriage, we separate and divorce. When we are not thankful for our children, we abuse and neglect them. When we are not thankful for our Bibles, they grow dusty and old. When we are not thankful for our churches, they grow empty and when we are not thankful for God's Son, Jesus, our hearts grow cold.

The other question that you may have been wondering about at the time you picked up the book – is why the book is set up in daily readings? Again, I'm glad you asked. If there is something we want to work on in our spiritual lives then we are going to get specific results when we work on that specific attribute. If it's love then love; if it's grace then grace; if it's thankfulness then thankfulness. Our focused study on one particular characteristic will bring forth focused results in that area. For this study it is thankfulness. Now if you don't want to work on thankfulness then go back to question one and if you're still not convinced then this is probably not the book for you. Just as bench presses won't help your abs this book isn't going to do a lot of good if you're trying to understand love better. But if you're interested in learning about how to be more thankful - well now we're talking.

The next reason that the book is split up into daily readings is because it creates consistency. If you create a period of consistency and focus by doing daily readings, I believe that God will help you to make great progress in being more thankful, and we hope to learn how to be thankful in everything at all times. Hopefully, these daily readings will be easy to read and provide a life giving opportunity for you to grow in your walk with God.

The final reason the book has been written in a daily format is because it is much easier to grow in your walk with God when you walk with someone else. These readings are much more impactful when shared with a spouse, a friend, a small group or your church.

My pastor has commented that when our church reads books together, it galvanizes vision. It brings unity and focus, and focused attention brings focused results that provide an atmosphere for the miraculous. As Jesus said, *"For where two or three have gathered together in My name, I am there in their midst"* (Matthew 18:20). (NASB)

Before you begin your journey, please note that this book is written in the first person voice even though both Michelle and I have authored the book. It was more consistent to write it that way and we believe easier to understand as well. There are parts of the book that each of us have written individually, but don' t worry about who wrote what part because we know that God united us together as one and the experiences we' ve gone through have been as one.

It is our prayer as you read this book, that God will minister to you, that you will consistently grow and become more thankful, and that by the end of this study you will be able to say with Paul in Philippians 4:12b, *"I have learned the secret of being content in any and every situation."* (NIV)

GIVING THANKS FROM YOUR *H*EART

Day 1: Introduction & Pride/Humility

Axis / Allies

When I was in my first year of college, my roommates introduced me to a very time consuming and competitive dice game called Axis and Allies. The Axis powers were the enemies from WWII, Germany and Japan, and the Allies were the US, UK and the USSR. It was kind of like Risk on steroids, but I'm not necessarily recommending it because it was so addictive. So instead of studying I'd be up late playing Axis and Allies (sorry mom and dad). Though the Axis powers and Allies are no longer enemies, the analogy fits for our study of thankfulness. There are enemies of a thankful heart and there are allies of a thankful heart – some things that will help you have a thankful heart and some things that will make it more difficult for you to be thankful. So I'd like to look at how each of these traits in our lives are Axis or Allies and how they affect our ability to be thankful.

Think of it as a "thank bank." Every time you think or act like one of the axis qualities you're removing coins from your thank bank. But every time you think or act like one of the allies of thankfulness, you're depositing coins into your thank bank. The more coins you have in your bank the more likely you are to be thankful. For example, the topics for the 1st day of this week are pride, which is the axis, and humility, which is the ally. If you say or do something prideful, imagine that you had to take a coin out of your bank. On the other hand, if you say or do something humble, then imagine putting a coin in your thank bank and see how you're doing at the end of each day. This is not a legalistic exercise, however, where you have to keep track with tally marks for you and your spouse. It's just to help you think about how these characteristics affect your thankfulness.

Now that exercise is just for fun. But the one that I would like you to take seriously this week is for you to try not to say thank you. Yes, you heard me correctly. Try not to say thank you. I've found that so often it is just a habit that we have been taught. Often when I've said it in the past, I just said it. I didn't think about what I said, and didn't really even mean it. Don't get me wrong. It's a good habit and my wife and I insist that our children maintain this habit. But the goal is not to get them to say it. It's to get them to mean it. So this week as you get your coffee or drop off your kids or pick up your paperwork don't say thank you. Instead just say a little thank you in your heart to God who hears that anyway. Now I will say that if you're in a situation that you think someone else might think you're being rude if you don't say it, then by all means this is not meant to be legalistic. It's simply an exercise to get you to think about what you're saying and to help you be thankful from your heart and not just from your mouth. It's only for a week and you'll have another simple assignment for next week so give it a shot and see what God can do.

Pride/Humility

Pride

I still remember it like it was yesterday. We had just moved to the New Orleans area to be a part of this dynamic church. I was sure that

God would open up a door for me to be in full time ministry because I knew that's what God had called me to do. So when that didn't happen, I was disappointed to say the least. I questioned everything, including my calling to full time ministry. So I decided to humble myself and fast, which I do whenever I want to hear from the Lord. I just wish I could hear better so I didn't have to fast so much. I needed an answer to the question of whether He had called me to full time ministry or not. With about a week left in the fast, God spoke wonderfully to me and confirmed my calling to full time ministry. On the last day of my fast, I went to the Christian bookstore to do some studying and to come before the Lord. Honestly, I was expecting to hear more sweet and pleasant words about being in full time ministry. However, I was rocked to the core when I heard so clearly God say,

"Yes, you're called to full time ministry, but what are you going to do about your pride?"

Needless to say, God got my attention. Pride is one of those things that the world embraces because it exudes confidence. The world teaches us to be proud. Be proud of your accomplishments; be proud of your heritage; be proud of yourself; be confident in yourself; believe in yourself and say good things to yourself and you will succeed. Pride makes you believe you are right – and have the right to whatever it is that will make you happy. Pride makes you believe you are superior, and no matter who gets hurt, it's your decisions that control your ultimate happiness. A great example of this was David. David allowed pride to convince him he deserved the beautiful Bathsheba. That pride led him first to commit adultery, then to commit murder. His pride blinded him until the prophet Nathan came and pointed it out. God's Word is clear about the destruction pride can cause. Proverbs 16:18-19 says, *"Pride goes before destruction, and a haughty spirit before a fall. Better to be of a humble spirit with the lowly, than to divide the spoil with the proud.*" (NKJV) There is nothing wrong with being confident, it just depends what or who you are confident in. "*Some trust in chariots and some in horses, but we trust in the name of the Lord our God*" (Psalm 20:7). (NIV) We need to remember our trust is in the Lord and our ultimate happiness and joy come from him.

So how do we guard our hearts from pride and live a truly thankful life? John MacArthur says in his sermon Spirit-Filled Thanksgiving, "there's only one kind of person who can be thankful for everything, and that's a humble person. That's right, that's a humble person. Well you say, what do you mean by that? Just this, listen, a humble person knows he doesn't deserve anything, right? So the smallest thing for him is a cause of thanksgiving. If you have a problem in your life being thankful the problem is not a lack of thanksgiving, that's the symptom the problem is pride. You're saying, God I just can't be thankful because I think I'm not getting what I deserve, see. But if you know you deserve nothing, if you see yourself as a sinner for whom nothing is really deserved then for anything that God would give you there could be nothing but thanks, see. It's really a pride problem. A thankful person always has a humble heart." "*God opposes the proud but gives grace to the humble*" (James 4:6b). (NIV) I don't know about you, but I want the Lord on my side. "*If God is for us, who can be against us*" (Romans 8:31). (NIV) Even David, who after committing murder seemed unworthy of God's grace, humbled himself in repentance before God. And God in His grace forgave him and used David for the purposes of His kingdom.

Humility

According to Webster's dictionary, humble means "not proud or arrogant; modest: low in importance, status or condition; lowly." The Bible defines humility this way: *"Do nothing out of selfish ambition or vain conceit, but in humility consider others better than yourselves. Each of you should look not only to your own interests, but also to the interests of others. Your attitude should be the same as that of Christ Jesus: Who, being in very nature God, did not consider equality with God something to be grasped, but made himself nothing, taking the very nature of a servant, being made in human likeness. And being found in appearance as a man, He humbled himself and became obedient to death— even death on a cross"* (Philippians 2:3-8). (NIV)

I used to think that humility was like a personality trait that either you were or you weren't. After I really started studying humility and working on my pride, I came to an important conclusion for my life and my walk with God. I started to study Philippians 2 and in verse 8 it says *"and being found in appearance as a man, he humbled himself and became obedient to death-even death on a cross."* (NIV) He humbled himself. All of a sudden it hit me like it never had before that Jesus humbled himself and it was possible for me to humble myself. There are a lot of different ways that I have tried to implement that in my own life and I could do a lot better, but the important revelation that I needed was that it was **possible,** and it wasn't just a personality trait that I had or I didn't have.

Gary Smalley recently did a marriage conference at our church. On his session on humility one of his visual aids was a sign, similar to what you would see a homeless person holding up. Only his sign didn't say "homeless" or "will work for food." It said "Helpless." It was a powerful visual reminder of how to humble ourselves. We need to remind ourselves that we are helpless before our God in heaven.

There is no better person to study when learning about humility than Jesus. He had more to be proud of than anyone yet He humbled himself lower than anyone. Everything about the love story from God, the entire life of Christ, is about serving others and putting on a life of humility. Isn't it ironic that it was the pride of the religious leaders that led them to crucify Jesus? Not only did He have the highest position, but He took on the lowest form. If you need to implement humility in your own life, just study Jesus and where He came from (Heaven), what He had (position), what He gave up (glory), and what He did on earth (serve). You will start to get a glimpse of what it means to be humble. When you are humble, you are thankful. Thankful because you don't deserve what you have. Thankful because you did not gain what you've got, and thankful because you did not grab what's been given.

Dear God, please help me to put down pride and to put on humility. Help me to realize that I am utterly helpless and totally dependant upon you. Please give me the mind of Christ about humility.

Review & Begin Weekly Activity

Day 2: Expectation/ Faith

Expectation

I was originally thinking about titling this section "Turning Entitlement into Grace," but God has been speaking to me about this word expectation and how it is different from faith. The definition of expectation is "something expected; often, a prospect of future benefit or fortune." And of course *"faith is being sure of what we hope for and certain of what we do not see"* (Hebrews 11:1). (NIV) Expectations are dangerous. They are dangerous because any time we get things stuck in our head that something must happen a certain way in a particular amount of time, we may be taking God's ability to be God out of the equation. For example, if we are believing God for a car, and our expectation is for a white Altima by the end of the week, if God wants to bless us with a blue Civic at the end of the month, we may miss God's plan completely. If we limit God to our time frame and our specifics, we may altogether miss the blessings God gives us simply because His time frame and specifics don't match our expectation. We may not even see that God has something else in mind for us.

I'm not saying that you can't use the word expectation or that it's wrong to have certain expectations. It is just something that we need to be very careful about if we want to have a thankful heart. What happens when we have expectations is that we take God out of the equation, and we are not allowing God to be God so that He can move how and when He pleases. I do believe in being specific with God, but when we ask for things in specific time frames, we limit God and may miss Him altogether.

For example, I had an opportunity to change careers and move from the retail industry into the restaurant business. There are a lot of similarities but there are also some differences as well. When I was approached about the opportunity and they were trying to recruit me, they told me about all the money I could make. For the sake of ease let's say it was $100,000. At that time that was a ton of money to me. I was only making about $30,000 annually and I was delivering newspapers for extra money as well. It was really a no brainier and we decided that my training pay, again just for sake of the example, would be $60,000. Everything was going along well and I finished training. They continued to pay me more money and I was making about $75,000 (for example). The only issue was my **expectation** was that I was going to make $100,000. So I became ungrateful. I couldn't see that God was miraculously providing and blessing our family with what I was making. I wanted my expectations to be met and my attitude showed it. I told them I was disappointed with how things were going and that I wanted to look around for another job. Well, they didn't wait for me to leave. They decided they were going to bring somebody in and replace me before I could leave them.

Expectations are very dangerous because they blind us to what else is going on around us. Expectations say, "It's my way or the highway." Expectations cause you to believe that you're entitled to something. Anytime you catch yourself thinking, "I earned it," "I deserve it" or "I did it" - beware. You could have an expectation that is stealing your ability to give thanks.

Again, there is nothing wrong with being specific with God, because that is how we can most easily see God at work in answering prayers. At the same time, when we are too specific or demanding about our way and our time, we may be seeking God's hand and not His face. God is not a genie who grants wishes. He is a loving Father who wants to bless you, and more often than not He will bless you in a different way than you are expecting. But that's ok because so often God's blessings are better than our wishes anyway. We have to remember that God is bigger than our box that we put Him in.   I think sometimes when we pray and make demands, or when we insist on answered prayer by such and such a date or time, God just chuckles because we don't know any better. Ultimately, we must lay the expectations of our time frames and our demands at His feet and exercise our faith.

Faith

As I sit here pondering about what faith is on one of the most gorgeous spring days down here in Southern Louisiana, I am so thankful for this moment with my youngest daughter Lydia. The sun is brightly shining; the water from the lake front gently breaks against the sea wall making a melodic rhythm as the birds are singing in the background. The wind is gently blowing to keep the temperature perfect. I asked my daughter what faith means to her and I thought about Jesus' comment that we must have faith like a little child to enter into the kingdom of heaven. She said that faith is courage. Courage is probably a great word when contrasting it with expectations. When we have expectations, we move forward in situations because we expect certain things to happen as a result of our actions. When we have faith, we move forward without knowing the outcome and by surrendering our expectations. In this manner, we don't know what the result will be, but we move forward anyway and that takes courage.

As I write this book, I must surrender the expectations that I have and leave the results up to God. All I know is that if I had One

Month To Live, (by Kerry & Chris Shook) I would want to be writing this book. If nothing else, this book writing project will cause thankfulness to grow and prosper in my wife's and my life, and we will have a great story to pass on to our children and the generations that follow. Without expectations, it takes faith to forge ahead not knowing what the outcome will be, but to trust in the plan that God has for us.

Forging ahead and trusting God's plan has become the unofficial motto of our family. In fact, our family verse is Proverbs 3:5-6: *"Trust in the LORD with all your heart and lean not on your own understanding; in all your ways acknowledge him, and he will make your paths straight."* (NIV) As I write this book, not only are we trusting God with it, we are trusting God – in the midst of an economic recession - to provide $6,000 for mission trips, and we are trusting God to direct us about moving to New Orleans. As a family, this means daily praying for God's provision and guidance, seeking Him by reading His word, fasting, surrendering our wants and desires (or expectations) and being willing and open to do whatever He asks. This truly takes courage. For mission trips, stepping out to commit to travel to an unknown land where our comfort zone is definitely challenged takes courage. Uprooting our family from great schools, a nice house and friends, to move into a city known for its high crime rate takes courage. But what we have learned, over and over and over again, is that standing in the center of God's will where we sometimes need to stand in courage – is so much better than standing outside of God's will where life might seem more safe. The will of God will never take you to where the grace of God will not protect you.

We recently finished a sermon series at our church called Uncommon Faith, and my pastor taught about the difference between natural faith and supernatural or uncommon faith. One of the best points he made in the series was that it is not our faith that changes things; it is our faith in God that changes things. We can have our faith in many different things, but only faith in God will do. When we have faith in our faith, then our expectations are ruling and we are trying to control the outcome. But when our faith or trust is in God, we surrender our expectations, lay down our agenda and put the results in the hands of a loving God who has plans to prosper us and not to harm us. You can trust Him – "faith" Him today.

Lord I surrender all of my expectations to you. I pray that you would give me the faith to trust You and Your ways at a whole new level. I'm sorry for all the times I demanded that You answer my prayers in my way. Give me eyes to see and ears to hear Your plans for my life.

Day 3: Security / Grace

Security

You may be wondering how security could be an enemy of a thankful heart. After all, isn't security a good thing? Wouldn't we be thankful if we knew our future was secure? Jesus put it this way in Luke 12:16-21 *"Then he spoke a parable to them saying: 'The ground of a certain rich man yielded plentifully. And he thought within himself, saying, 'What shall I do, since I have no room to store my crops? So he said, 'I will do this: I will pull down my barns and build greater, and there I will store all my crops and my goods. And I will say to my soul, 'Soul, you have many goods laid up for many years; take your ease; eat, drink, and be merry.' But God said to him, 'Fool! This night your soul will be required of you; then whose will those things be which you have provided?' 'So is he who lays up treasure for himself, and is not rich toward God.' "* (NKJV)

Jesus didn't say that there was anything wrong with being wealthy, it was simply a matter of how the wealth was viewed. I certainly want to be able to provide for my family and, as the Bible says, to provide for the generations that follow. God wants us to prosper and God wants us to enjoy what He provides for us. 1Timothy 6:17 says, *"Command those who are rich in this present world not to be arrogant nor to put their hope in wealth, which is so uncertain, but to put their hope in God, who richly provides us with everything for our enjoyment."* (NIV) It really comes down to motive, because if your motive is to provide for your family, to be rich in good deeds, and you're willing to share generously, then you're on the right track. But if your motive is accumulation and security, then it is probably stealing your thankfulness.

If there was a picture of your hand holding your finances, what would it look like? Would your hand be closed and tight fisted trying to hold on to whatever you've got, or would it be an open hand ready to receive and willing to give at the same time? Think about how both postures make you feel. One posture maintains the attitude of scarcity and lack, holding on for dear life what you don't want to lose. The other posture maintains an attitude of abundance and a confidence knowing that everything you have comes from God.

Let's take a moment to compare two different life styles. Living to get and living to give. Living to get means your primary concern is accumulation. You are simply trying to get as much as you can, and hold on to what you already have to try and maintain some semblance of security for yourself. There is always a justification for gaining more and even better ones for keeping it. One of the Bible characters that probably had this type of mentality was the rich young ruler (Matthew 19:16-22). He came to Jesus and asked what he must do to inherit the kingdom of God. Jesus knew what his heart was attached to, so He told him to sell all his possessions, give them to the poor and come and follow Him. This was it. This was his big chance. He could have been the 13th disciple. I wonder how many other people Jesus asked to come and follow Him, but refused because their heart was attached to something else? In any event, the Bible tells us that the rich young ruler went away sad because he couldn't bring himself to give up his possessions. Not that Jesus' expectation is that you put the book down, go sell everything you have and give it to the poor. We've already seen that the criterion is whether you are rich toward God. This is an example of someone that was living to get, and he couldn't part with what he had because it meant more to him than his relationship with Jesus.

On the other hand, living to give means that you are open to the opportunity and possibility of giving yourself and your finances to God and His purposes. It means that instead of always being concerned about yourself and how you will live or survive without this or that, you have a concern for others and their needs. One of the Biblical examples we have of this type of person is in the story of the widow's mites (Luke 21:1-4). Here we have a very poor widow who gives a very small offering when compared monetarily with what everyone else was giving. Jesus pulls His disciples aside and points out that the widow gave more than everyone because she gave all she had. Her sacrifice was greater than the others who gave more. She knew it was more blessed to give than to receive, and God recognized her sacrifice. Again, Jesus isn't asking you to give all that you have, but it is this type of attitude that lives to give and isn't focused on what you're going to get. It's on the Giver of all gifts. The Bible tells us the rich young ruler walked away sad. I'd like to think that as Jesus and the disciples watched the widow walk away that there was a smile on her face, and that she walked away in joy knowing that she had given her best. How do you want to walk away from your encounter with Jesus? Give up the security of your finances and depend on the security of your loving Heavenly Father as you give your very best. It is my prayer that the joy of the Lord will comfort your soul and bring a smile to your face as you do his will.

How are you holding your hand? Especially during more difficult financial times, the natural reaction is to start to hold on tighter to the possessions you have and find new ways to accumulate more. But that is exactly the opposite of how we should approach tough financial times. It's all God's money anyway, and as soon as our fingers start to close to grasp what we have, our heart begins to close with it. In fact, *if you look at the picture of your hand, it may just correspond with the openness of your heart.* If you let your fingers close on your possessions, then your heart will begin to close toward God. But if you continue to live with an open hand, then your heart will consequently remain open to God and how He wants to use you and your possessions to serve Him. You will then understand that what you have is not meant for your security, because the only reason you have it, is the grace of God.

Grace

We usually apply the term grace to our relationship with God. This is very good and necessary, but what we don't realize sometimes is that **all** we have is the grace of God. Every talent, every dime, every ability, every good thing that you can do or have is from God and supplied by His grace. *"Every good and perfect gift is from above"* (James 1:17a). (NIV) That's what the Bible says. You mean my business that I've built from the ground up and worked at my whole life...you mean my creative ability for entertaining...you mean my keen business sense and ability to make deals...you mean my ability to teach and communicate...you mean (you fill in the blank)? YES! It is all the grace of God. If it's good, it came from God – period. Even Paul said if it wasn't for the grace of God he wouldn't have accomplished anything. All he did was work hard. That was it. *"But by the grace of God I am what I am, and His grace to me was not without effect. No, I worked harder than all of them—yet not I, but the grace of God that was with me"* (1Cor 15:10). (NIV) When your hand is open and you realize that all you have is truly the grace of God, you will be so thankful for all that you have because you will realize you didn' t earn it. You wouldn' t have it without God and it' s all His anyway.

Grace is a funny thing because it doesn' t take away your responsibility, it simply removes your rights. It removes your right to be greedy, it removes your right to accumulate for yourself and your purposes, but it retains your responsibility to steward over the good things that God has given you. The deeper your understanding of God' s grace in your life, the greater capacity you will have for thankfulness. It makes sense because grace means you don' t deserve something. When you don' t deserve something and you get it anyway, you are much more thankful for it, than if you feel that you' ve earned it. Therefore, the more you see the grace of God at work in your lives the more thankful you will be.

My oldest daughter Kaley was especially thankful when she saw the movie High School Musical 3. Of course all of our girls are huge fans and so it seemed like a pretty good punishment to not allow Kaley to see High School Musical 3 in the movie theatres when it came out. That was until I decided that I wanted to teach her a very important lesson. I originally thought I was going to teach her a lesson about the consequences of her actions. But this lesson wasn' t going to be a "this hurts me more than it' s going to hurt you" lesson. (We' ve had plenty of those.) God put it on my heart to teach her about the grace of God. I know some of you are thinking that I just caved and she' s got me wrapped around her little finger, but it wasn' t like that. She wasn' t pouting or complaining or trying to manipulate her way out of her punishment. Surprisingly, she was handling it rather well on the outside. So I thought it would be a good time to show her that we don' t always get what we deserve and I took her to the movie theater and surprised her with going to High School Musical 3. When she asked why, I made it very clear to her that she didn't deserve it; but that I was showing her grace and we were going to the movie anyway.   She was very thankful and appreciative, and I hope that she learned a very important lesson about receiving and extending the grace of God.

It is my hope and prayer as you consider the differences between gaining security for yourself and being rich toward God, that you will have a renewed sense of God's grace in your life, and no matter what circumstances you find yourself in you will be open handed and open hearted.   In Matthew 6:33 Jesus says,   *"But seek first the kingdom of God and His righteousness, and all these things shall be added to you."* (NKJV)   Jesus communicated this important principle in two different ways: one in a parable in which he summarized it by saying that we are to be rich toward God and in the other he spoke plainly and stated to seek God and his purposes first. Our life is not our own and neither are our gifts, talents or resources. It is all Gods.   Open up your hand to the God of all mercy and grace and taste and see that He is good.   As you open up your hand to God you will see that as you give, it will be given to you in a good measure, pressed down, shaken together and running over (Luke 6:38).

I pray the following parable will be a theme that runs throughout your life.   The stocks of a certain rich man produced a good return.   He thought to himself,   "What shall I do, I don't even need any more money?"   Then he said,   "This is what I will do. I'll ask God what He would like me to do with the money since it's His money anyway, for who knows what tomorrow will bring?"   Then he said,   "This is what I'll do. I'll take this money and start a home for underprivileged kids.   I will be rich toward God and store up treasures in heaven."   Then no matter what tomorrow brings, you will be able to stand before God with joy in your heart and a smile on your face.

Dear Lord, please open up my eyes to see Your grace on my life. Please help me to live for You and Your kingdom, and not for myself and my possessions. Lord, I want You to be proud of me. Show me how to use what You've given me to honor You, so that I can walk away with Your joy filling my heart. Lord, I open up my hand to You today, in Jesus Name, Amen.

Day 4: Impatience/Patience

Impatience

You may be wondering what impatience has to do with being ungrateful. If you are impatient, then you are usually not content with your current circumstances. Whether you' re sitting behind a school bus or waiting for the longest light in town to turn green, if you are impatient then you are not satisfied with your current situation and you want it to change. This also applies to more important life happenings than just traffic. Please don' t feel like I' m just out to get you by preaching about impatience, because I have had a lot of type A tendencies where I wanted immediate results. Of course, our society doesn' t help it any with microwaves, drive thrus and instant everything.

I remember when we broke the curse of impatience in our family. I had been really impatient about some things in my life. One of the things that my wife and I had always been impatient about was with her pregnancies and the birth of our children. Our first three children were girls. With every one of them we tried to find out their gender as soon as possible and we never made it to the due date. We would do everything we could to make the baby come early; walking a lot, driving over bumps and taking a trip to the hospital every time the baby kicked in the last trimester. I think for most of the girls the hospitals just got tired of seeing us and decided to just put Michelle into labor. So with our fourth child we decided that we were going to break the curse of impatience and we weren' t going to find out the gender. We were going to try our very best not to go before the due date. Of course you can find out the gender and there are reasons for having a baby before the due date. But for us that is what we needed to do at that time. To our great surprise, and even though we had all kinds of people tell us that chances were we were going to have another girl, God blessed us with a wonderful baby boy. I don't think that God blessed us with a boy because of our patience, but it sure did make it a better surprise.

One of the things I've learned about impatience is that it can rob us of the blessings of God. What I mean by that is when we are impatient and we grab what hasn't been given to us, it may serve our purposes but God may have had something better waiting for us that we never knew about. One of the ways that impatience manifests itself is in the spirit of deal making. When you're always looking for a better deal you may miss the best deal that God has waiting for you. *It's not a question of how good a deal you get, it's a question of whether it's God's deal.* In the past I have even been guilty of making deals with God. You know the kind where you want something really badly, so you try and force God's hand by saying, "God if you do this one thing for me than I'll do this for you." This is really a manifestation of impatience where you try and get your way with God, as if you could ever bribe God. You have probably heard that God is more concerned about your character than your comfort, which is very true, but I tell you with regard to patience that God is more concerned about your friendship than He is about your fulfillment. So if you find yourself working on being more patient, God might just be trying to work on your friendship.

Patience

Patience is a virtue. How many times have you heard that in your life? What makes me cringe is that the only way I know to get more patience is by having opportunities to work on it. At times in the past I have avoided asking God for patience because I know He answers prayer, and I really didn' t want Him to answer that one. In all seriousness, I have become very aware of my need for more patience. I don' t want any more opportunities to have it, but I do want to take advantage of becoming more patient every chance I get.

Abraham is one of the best examples of patience in the Old Testament. When God came to Abraham and promised to make him a great nation, and that his descendants would inherit the land, Abraham was 75 years old. Abraham didn' t have his first child with his wife until he was 100. He waited 25 years for the promise of his son. Talk about patience. That would make anyone patient. Of course he had his struggles, who wouldn' t waiting 25 years for a promise, but the Bible says, *"for he waited for the city which has foundations, whose builder and maker is God"* (Hebrews 11:10). (NKJV) Romans 4:18 says about Abraham,

> *" who, contrary to hope, in hope believed, so that he became the father of many nations, according to what was spoken, 'So shall your descendents be.' And not being weak in faith, he did not consider his own body, already dead (since he was about a hundred years old) and the deadness of Sarah' s womb. He did not waver at the promise of God through unbelief, but was strengthened in faith, giving glory to God, and being fully convinced that what He had promised He was also able to perform."* (NKJV)

So you can see Abraham didn' t take his promise and put in on a shelf like it never happened. He believed that promise and grew in patience as he waited for its fulfillment. Patience is not accomplished by stopping your belief in the promises of God. *Patience is created in the tension of the now and the not yet.* The now is the promise you are holding onto, for healing or salvation for loved ones or any other promises of God. The not yet is the reality in the natural world that the promise hasn't yet been fulfilled. It is within this tension and time frame of the now and the not yet that patience is built.

James 1:2 *"My brethren, count it all joy when you fall into various trials, knowing that the testing of your faith produces patience. But let patience have its perfect work, that you may be perfect and complete lacking nothing."* (NKJV)

Galatians 6:9 *"And let us not grow weary while doing good, for in due season we shall reap if we do not lose heart."* (NKJV)

Hebrews 10:34ff *"....for you had compassion on me in my chains, and joyfully accepted the plundering of your goods, knowing that you have a better and an enduring possession for yourselves in heaven. Therefore do not cast away your confidence, which has great reward. For you have need of endurance, so that after you have done the will of God, you may receive the promise: 'For yet a little while, And He who is coming will come and will not tarry. Now the just shall live by faith; But if anyone draws back, My soul has no pleasure in him.' But we are not of those who draw back to perdition, but of those who believe to the saving of the soul."* (NKJV)

The message of these verses is don't quit, don't give up, and don't stop believing. This is the only thing that can cancel out the promises of God in your life. *"Yet those who wait for the Lord will gain new strength; they will mount up with wings like eagles, they will run and not get tired, they will walk and not become weary."* (Isaiah 40:31). (NASB) I understand what it's like to want to quit and give up, but don't do it. Help is on the way.

I remember when I was working at a 24 hour diner as my first real job after my back surgery. It sounded like a great opportunity, the training went well and then bam! I got thrown into my own store with unrealistic expectations, a difficult supervisor, working about 80 hours a week, and having to pull a 20 hour shift about once a week near the end. It took every ounce of strength in my body not to quit. I had wonderful encouragement from my wife, and a great man who was discipling me, who told me I couldn't quit. I was looking for a new job as best I could with my wife helping me. I remember coming home from work, and just to be nice my wife would ask me how work was that day. I would respond by saying, "Well, I didn't quit!" Those were very good days – the days I made it without quitting! When you are going through very difficult circumstances and discouraging times, you are doing great if you can say, "I didn't quit, I didn't stop believing, I didn't give up hope." If you have given up, God is right there forgiving and restoring you, but it is when you don't give up that your faith produces patience.

Lord, forgive my impatience and ungracious attitude. Grow my faith as I press ahead in the race of life. Thank you that You don't give me more than I can handle. Help me to remember Your yoke is easy and Your burden is light as I learn to be patient, especially during the trials that may come. Remind me daily, Lord that You are in control and Your timing is perfect.

Day 5: Discontentment/Contentment

Discontentment

In today's society, many people are increasingly discontent. Society portrays the message that money, health and success are the answer to discontentment. However, Americans have more money and material things and are generally in better health than many other nations in our world. Yet, few are content. The young and the old, the rich and the poor, are restless, dissatisfied, and discontent.

My wife had the privilege of traveling to Cambodia in 2008 for a mission trip. One of the things that touched her the most was the happiness and contentment of the Khmer people. In the small village where she ministered, the families lived in one room cement houses, without the conveniences of indoor plumbing and ceiling fans. They lived in dirty, hot conditions that would be appalling to so many of us. However, their appreciation and contentment touched all the people on the trip. By our standards, we wouldn't even consider their living arrangements a house. 1 Timothy 6:6-8 says *"But godliness with contentment is great gain. For we brought nothing in to the world, and we can take nothing out of it. But if we have food and clothing, we will be content with that."* (NIV)

This verse doesn't even say anything about having a house, just food and clothing. How many of us would be content without a house? I'm not suggesting that you sell your house and become homeless in order to find contentment. It's not that great. After hurricane Katrina we lost the place we were living in and we needed to find another one. We didn't feel like we were supposed to move away from the area, but there was literally no place to live. Everyone who lost their houses in the city moved out to the suburbs and there were hundreds of applications for one place to live. We lived with friends for a time so that we didn' t have to leave the area. Then God miraculously opened a door for us to stay in an affordable apartment when everyone and their brother were looking for a place to live.

Thinking about not having a house to live in does make us pause about what it means to be content, and what it looks like to be discontent. When I was growing up, my dad was a very successful banker and we had a nice home and nice things. We never really lacked for anything and there was very little I wanted that I didn' t get. I' m not saying we grew up in a mansion with a butler and a maid, but from my perspective, and compared to the other kids at school, we led comfortable lives. In some way, I think it contributed to a spirit of discontentment inside of me. My parents did a great job raising us and they tried not to spoil us. They made sure we got jobs and worked during the summers, and we always did chores. Still, I knew we had money and somewhere along the way I became discontent. It became a joke in my house at Christmas that when someone got me a present, I opened it and they would say "we know that one' s going back." I became very picky about everything, not out of necessity but because of my preferences. I said thank you for my gifts and appeared to be thankful, but my actions said something else entirely. I was at the mall the next day taking back everything everyone had gotten me, and I was getting what I wanted. I' ll still take things back if they don' t fit or for some other reason, but if it' s a preference issue, I' m going to keep it and be thankful for it. A couple of years ago after my back surgery, we had a friend of ours give us a fairly new Saturn Vue. At the time we only had one fully functioning vehicle and we were awed by this gift and God's graciousness. The only problem was that it had a stick shift and I didn't know how to drive a standard. I tried to learn, but what I didn't recognize at the time was that there was a discontentment in me. The vehicle was such a blessing and I began to use it to deliver pizzas while my back healed. Every once in a while my back would bother me a little bit when I shifted gears. I talked to my spiritual counsel at church, and his wise suggestion was to just continue on while my back healed. I did that and we kept the vehicle for another year, and it was such a blessing to our family. Then we had a building drive at our church and I really wanted to give the vehicle away. Gas prices were rising and I was thinking I was going to start commuting further to work. I was thinking about getting something with better gas mileage anyway, so I talked with my wife about it and we decided to go ahead and do it. I got the title and put it in the other person's name and brought him the keys on one of the pledge nights for the building.

The only issue was that the pastors of the church knew that my family and I were in need of that vehicle and they wisely had the person give it back to us. Since we were talking about getting another vehicle anyway, we decided that we would try and sell it. We took out an ad in the paper and included it in one of those car magazines. This is when gas prices were through the roof and the economy really started to tank. In case you didn't know, nobody was buying SUV's then. The whole time we had the vehicle for sale, I don't think we got one phone call. That is when it hit me - God had given me this vehicle and had picked it out especially for me and I was trying to politely return it and tell Him that I wanted something else. I was not satisfied. Although I kept saying we were thankful, I wasn't truly content and was portraying an ungrateful attitude.

Contentment

One secret to being content is to focus on God and His strength. It sounds simple, but let me tell you what I mean. My favorite verse of scripture for longer than I can remember has been Philippians 4:11-13: *"I am not saying this because I am in need, for I have learned to be content whatever the circumstances. I know what it is to be in need, and I know what it is to have plenty. I have learned the secret of being content in any and every situation, whether well fed or hungry, whether living in plenty or in want. I can do everything through him who gives me strength."* (NIV)

Although this has been my favorite verse for who knows how long, I haven't thought much about this secret that Paul talks about. A secret is important. A secret is vital information and Paul says in this verse that he has learned the secret of being content. Shh, don't tell anybody the secret is that Paul found his strength from God and not from the circumstances or the people in his life. He said that he knew what it was to be content whether he had a lot or a little, because his focus and attention was not on his possessions, it was on God. Paul had an eternal perspective that earth was not his home – heaven was. Over and over again we see this truth throughout Paul's writings and the New Testament. Set your minds on things above, our citizenship is in heaven, etc. etc. When we have an eternal perspective, then our hope will be in God and not in man or the things of man. It gets really simple then. Jesus is the same yesterday, today and forever and He said He would never leave you or forsake you.

My pastor recently told about a trip he took to Nigeria. Upon entering, he had to show his passport because he wasn't a citizen of that country. He is a citizen of the United States and was just visiting

Nigeria. The same is true of our time here on earth. When we realize that this is not our home, and we are citizens of heaven, then it becomes very easy to be content with what we have because it doesn' t matter any way. We can' t take it with us and it doesn' t transfer over to any treasures in heaven, no matter how much stuff we accumulate or how good our stuff is. We can' t take it with us and it won' t matter one bit when we get to heaven. Whoever dies with the most stuff still dies, and their stuff still rusts and decays. Paul was content just to spend time with God and to do his will. Paul found the secret of being content by spending time with the giver of all secrets, and keeping his eyes focused on Him.

Another secret to being content comes in the form of *not* doing something. Just as there is great power in setting your face toward God and spending time with Him, there is also great power and freedom when we turn our attention and our focus away from the things of man. Hebrews 13:5-6 says *"Keep your lives free from the love of money and be content with what you have, because God has said, 'Never will I leave you; never will I forsake you.' So we say with confidence, 'The Lord is my helper; I will not be afraid. What can man do to me?' "* (NIV)

This is the same secret stated in Philippians 4, only in the converse. Just as contentment comes from being with God, we see that it does not come from concerning ourselves with the things of man. We can be content no matter what our circumstances because our hope is in God and not in man or the things of man. God can be trusted, He is always faithful, He always provides and He is always there. There is nothing that can be taken away from you and nothing that you can lose in God' s economy. Man can take away my job, man can take away my house, man can take away my money and man can take away my stocks, but I will not be afraid for the Lord is my helper.   *"God is our refuge and strength, an ever-present help in trouble"*   (Psalm 46:1). (NIV) *"Even though I walk through the valley of the shadow of death, I will fear no evil"* (Psalm 23:4a). (NIV)

If we want what man wants and we buy into all the commercials that show the latest and greatest of everything, we will lose our contentment. If we depend on man for our approval and we need to always talk about our accomplishments, then we will not be content. What we need to understand is that our success in life is not based on our prosperity, it is based on the decisions that we make and our obedience to Christ. It is not based on how we're doing financially compared to the Jones'. Our success in God's eyes is determined by the every day decisions we make about how we live our life and ultimately the condition of our heart. Our challenge isn't that we have a faulty definition of prosperity, it is that we have a faulty definition of success. If we make comparisons with man about what they have and about what we don't have, we will be discontented. If our focus is on God and not on man, then we won't want all the latest and greatest of everything. If we seek God's approval and not mans, we can be content with our lives even if they are not esteemed in the eyes of man. If we focus on thanking God for what we do have instead of worrying about what we don't have - we will have learned, like Paul, the secret of being content.

Dear God, Please help me to fix my eyes on You and the things that You are concerned about. Show me how to live in Your strength, to live for Your approval, and to be content about what I have. After all, You gave it to me. Thank You. Please give me Your strength to live in that secret place of being content.

Day 6: Envy/Applause

Envy

I' m not really proud of all these personal examples of characteristics that steal your thankfulness, but my prayer is that as I share these stories, you will be able to correct any of these characteristics in your own life before they cause you pain. As we address envy in our lives, we could just as easily talk about coveting, jealously or comparison. Envy is directed at another person while coveting is directed at what another person has. Jealousy usually has to do with what we don' t want others to have. Comparison is a very funny thing because it' s something that has become inherent and accepted in our culture. Whether it' s trying to keep up with the Jones' or most of the retail commercials we see, it is engrained in our heads that how we look and what we have is constantly compared with the newest and best of everything. We end up making comparisons constantly and we don' t even know it. We compare our clothes with those of the people we meet. We compare our houses with our neighbors' , and we compare our vehicles with our coworkers' .

My wife and I just purchased a very nice used van and we are very thankful for it. But as we recently drove on the highways of New Orleans, I noticed my sinful flesh comparing other mini vans with new car tags on the back windows. If it was nicer than ours I became envious, and if it was older than ours I became proud. My daughter Maddy told me today, "the devil is a liar and we should pray to God when the devil lies to us."   I mentioned to my wife what was happening and she confessed the same thing. What is it inside of us that compares all that we have and all that we are to whoever is in our proximity? We have got to realize that no good comes from comparing ourselves or our possessions with others. Paul warns against comparison in Galatians 6:4-5. *"Each one should test his own actions. Then he can take pride in himself, without comparing himself to somebody else, for each one should carry his own load."* (NIV)

Each of us needs to learn to be thankful for who we are and what we have. This is harder to do when we don' t have what we want, but that is exactly when it is the most important. If you are believing for a blue Civic and someone down the street from you gets a new blue Civic, beware. There is a temptation to be envious of that person. This happened to me when I was believing for a ministry position that someone else got. I became very envious and I didn' t even realize it. I verbally attacked this pastor under the guise of hearing from the Lord. When it happened, I wasn' t even conscious of my envy, but after repenting and seeking the Lord, He showed me that I was envious of this pastor. That is why comparison is so dangerous. It leads us to either pride or envy unless we step in and crush the cycle and begin to thank God for who we are and what we have. Life is not fair, but God is good and He is just. We must stop our sibling rivalries within the body of Christ and learn to unite by concerning ourselves with our own relationship with God and embracing the concept of applause.

Applause

If you think about the concept of applause, it is by its very nature meant for someone else. Applause was never meant for ourselves. It was always meant for others. When we applaud ourselves there is something unnatural about it. Applause is for others. When I played basketball in Bible College there was an inscription in the gym that has always stuck in my mind, "Humble in victory-Gracious in defeat." When we have victory we are to be humble, but when others have victory, blessings or rewards in their lives, then we are to applaud their efforts and encourage their spirits. Who are we to judge, and why should we ever be envious of any blessing or reward that anyone else receives? The only reason we would do that is if God had a limited supply of blessing or reward, and if someone else got some it meant that there was less for us. But God's resources are limitless. It is not in the shape of a pie and if someone else takes a piece there is less for us. God has all the pies. When we realize that God's resources are limitless and His rewards are not contained within the walls of a box, then we can applaud others because we realize that their blessing does not limit our opportunities. So maybe it's not that we need to limit our envy as much as we need to increase our belief in God and what He is capable of.

If you and your coworker are applying for the same promotion and your coworker gets it, your response should be to applaud and esteem that person because you believe that God could create another position just for you, or could even promote you over your coworker. The possibilities are limitless in the hand of God. God is not limited in His resources. He is only limited by your attitude. So whether we feel like it or not, we need to take every opportunity to applaud others as they meet success. A great Biblical example of this is the attitude the apostles had when hearing the testimony of the work done among the Gentiles. We see in Acts chapter 15 verses 3 and 4 that as Paul and Barnabas described their work among the Gentiles, it brought great joy to those who heard. It would have been very easy for the other apostles and followers of Christ to be jealous and envious of the great work God was allowing Paul and Barnabas to do among the Gentiles. Instead, they received that news with joy and applauded their work.

This concept of applauding others can be very challenging. It is especially hard for children to understand. The majority of their life is based on what is fair and not fair. My wife and I are very intentional about teaching our children the principles and characteristics that we know resemble those that Christ portrayed. If we can teach them such traits now, hopefully they will retain it throughout their lives.

When High School Musical 3 came out, my wife's and my initial plan had been for the ladies, my wife and three girls, to have a girl's night out and see the movie. For those of you with girls, you know what a big deal any of these movies are. However, my oldest daughter did something that warranted a hit to the heart type punishment – so she was "grounded" from seeing this movie. However, as you'll remember from day 3, God really showed me how I could tangibly help her understand the concept of grace, so I unexpectedly took her to see the movie. For my other two daughters, their response could have very easily been "That's not fair! Why did she get to see the movie and we didn't?" However, because we are constantly encouraging our children to be thankful for what they have, to speak words of encouragement and love to others, my other two daughters were very excited for Kaley that she got to see the movie. Were they disappointed? Of course. Did they express their disappointment? Of course, but they did it in a very gracious and appropriate way. The joy and excitement they showed for Kaley was a real lesson on applause for both my wife and me.

Though their responses are not always that heart warming, this time it was. We need to remember that even when it doesn't seem fair, or it seems virtually impossible, our words – our applause

‒ will warm the hearts of those receiving it. Isn' t that what it' s about? Warming hearts and showing love to others? Ultimately that is what our applause should be, an expression of love. Not just our love, but Christ' s love. Forget about what you don' t have, or what you want, and take a few minutes to think about who you could applaud today. God blesses each one of us because He loves us. God invites us as His followers to show that love to others. 1 Corinthians 8:1 says, "*Love edifies.*" Our words should be words that speak love and life to others, and that includes applauding and encouraging their success.

God help me to be thankful for the blessings You've given me, and not to focus on what others have. Help me not to compare myself with those around me, but to focus on my relationship with You. Help me to applaud others, lift others up, and be an encouragement to them.

Complete & Reflect On Weekly Activity

GIVING THANKS IN

EVERYTHING

Day 1: Introduction &
In Season And Out Of Season

Giving thanks in everything is sort of like unconditional love. Unconditional love says, it doesn't matter what the circumstances are it doesn't matter what you've done in the past or what you're going to do in the future – I love you anyway. Unconditional love is a choice – it's committed – it's intentional. Unconditional love is expressed in the traditional wedding vows that so many of us have used or are familiar with – in sickness and in health, for richer for poorer, until death do us part. The idea is that it doesn't matter what you can bring to the table, you are loved anyway. Unconditional love says that no matter what happens to you, I will love you. Giving thanks in everything is very similar to that because when we talk about giving thanks in everything, there has to be a realization that not everything in life will be pleasant. We have to realize that there will be times in our lives when we will not feel like being thankful. And we need to know that giving thanks in everything is not based on how we're feeling, just like unconditional love presses beyond our feelings and into the place of no conditions. There are no conditions on our thankfulness toward God. There may be adverse circumstances or unexplained accidents in our lives, but our choice remains to be thankful toward God – to give thanks in everything, at all times.

Sometimes you may be just moving along and bam, out of nowhere, you get hit in life. I remember when we were traveling cross country as a family, driving back from Michigan to Illinois, so that I could preach at one of my best friend's weddings. We had just stopped to get something to eat and were trying to get back to the expressway. As we were pulling out of the parking lot, we had to cross a busy street with four lanes and a median in the middle. I pulled out past the first two lanes of traffic into the median area, waiting for a chance to merge into oncoming traffic. Unfortunately for us, a truck came barreling down the street apparently trying to make the light. A car pulled out from the gas station, turned in front of him, and instead of hitting that vehicle, he swerved and smashed into our stationary vehicle, sending us spinning. We were just sitting there minding our own business and bam, we were hit.

Thankfully, no one had any major injuries even though the vehicle was totaled. The impact was primarily to the trunk of the car though if it had been one foot closer to the rear passenger door, our daughter Kaley may have been seriously injured or even killed. Even though our car was totaled and we didn't make the wedding, we were so thankful that everyone was alive after such a horrifying accident. We could have complained or stewed over our difficulties, but that doesn't do any good. In fact, *complaining is one of the fruits of an ungrateful heart.* Whenever you are tempted to complain, that is exactly when you need to turn your attitude around and choose to be thankful.

Sometimes in life we get hit by unexpected damage or heartache, and though it may be difficult, that is one of the most important times to be thankful. I'm not saying you need to be jumping up and down saying, "Thank you – thank you," but you can say "I don't understand it, I don't like it, but thank you, God, for sparing me." Thank God for what you have instead of despising what you don't have. It was our practice, and still is, before we leave on a trip to say a prayer and ask God to protect us and our vehicle, and to bless our trip. We had prayed before we left that day, and I remember Kaley, who was only about five at the time, asking why God let us get into an accident after we prayed. Oh, the faith of a child! There was an inconsistency in her mind. If God is a good God and He had the capability of protecting us, then why did we get into the car accident? I didn't really have an answer and I still don't. All I know is *"the thief comes only to steal and kill and destroy; I (Jesus) came that they may have life, and have it abundantly"* (John 10:9). (NASB) We may not always have the answers or the understanding, but God is still good and He's still on the throne. The devil may be trying to steal your joy or trying to stop God's good plans for your life, but always remember, it wasn't God that did it. God is not to blame. He didn't forget about you. He didn't lose track of you, and He still cares for you more than ever. Don't lose focus. Don't lose faith. God is still faithful. He always has been and He always will be.

Because some of the "accidents" in life are unexplainable, we need to be so careful about not judging others and the circumstances they are going through. Just because something bad happens to someone doesn't mean they were doing something wrong, or they needed to have more faith, etc. Sometimes life is just hard and sometimes it's tough. But that is exactly when you need to keep hope alive. That is when you need to choose to be thankful, even when you don't feel like it. That is when you need to *draw closer to God instead of blaming Him.* That is the time to keep believing, praying and confessing God's word and His blessings over your life. If for some unexplainable reason bad things happen, do your very best to give thanks in everything at all times.

One of the things that will help you to be thankful in everything is to count your blessings. Everyone has heard the expression, "count your blessings," but very few of us ever really do.   Here's your chance to really count your blessings.   Your assignment for this week is to make a list every day of what you're thankful for.   Just make a list each day before or after you read, whether it is a big list or a small list, whether it's just from that day, that year, or from your entire life.   Write some things each day that you're thankful for.   They can be big things like being thankful for your spouse, or they can be little things like a beautiful day.   See what God is doing in your life and look for things that you can be thankful for each day.   You may repeat from day to day, as long as you're writing them down so you don't forget.   After day six, review what you've written and see how your list has changed throughout the week, or look for something repeatedly written that you are especially thankful for.   You'll be surprised how much you have to be thankful for!

In Season and Out of Season

Ecclesiastes 3:1-8 says,

"There is a time for everything, and a season for every activity under heaven: a time to be born and a time to die, a time to plant and a time to uproot, a time to kill and a time to heal, a time to tear down and a time to build, a time to weep and a time to laugh, a time to mourn and a time to dance, a time to scatter stones and a time to gather them, a time to embrace and a time to refrain, a time to search and a time to give up, a time to keep and a time to throw away, a time to tear and a time to mend, a time to be silent and a time to speak, a time to love and a time to hate, a time for war and a time for peace." [NIV]

There is a time and season for everything. Time and chance happens to all. It really doesn' t matter what season of life you' re going through right now. Times may change and seasons may change, but God never changes. He is always the same yesterday, today and forever. He is always worthy of our praise. He is always to be worshiped and adored, and we should always give Him thanks. That doesn' t mean we have to thank Him **for** the rough times or **for** the miserable circumstances, but even in the midst of those circumstances, we need to find a way to be thankful toward Him.

As my wife and I write this book, we are in a season of nurturing our four children, ages 11, 8, 6 and 3. For those of you with young children, you know this season can be very rewarding, full of hugs and kisses one moment, yet full of frustration and challenge the next. For our particular family it' s a challenging season with four young children, me working a lot of nights and my wife working full time as well. Is this ideal for our family? No, but we know it' s just a season where we need to do what we have to in order to provide for our family. There are days when I don' t see my wife with her working days and me working nights. Surely, the kids aren' t going to have as good a summer as if their mom was home with them all day, but it' s just a season. In our season we thank God for our strong family unit, for His great provision, and for wonderful children that are flexible and well behaved; but most of all we thank Him for His grace that sustains, esteems, and blesses our family during this challenging time. We know it is only a season, we know we are not alone, and we have confident hope it will be better.

Ecclesiastes says there will be hard times in our lives: a time for death, a time to weep, a time to mourn, a time to give up, etc.; but Jesus said, "*take heart! I have overcome the world*" (John 16:33).(NIV) Even when hard times come and circumstances are difficult, hope is not lost. The circumstances in your life are not your determining factor. Jesus is the Lord of your life and when you look at your life and your circumstances through His eyes, things will look much different. This is difficult to do, but necessary. It's like being in the dark and all you can see is that you're suffering and having a difficult time, but seeing from Jesus' perspective is like having night vision goggles – you'll be able to see through your darkness through His greater light.

One thing you'll be able to see with your night vision goggles is that seasons don't last forever. Genesis 8:22 says, "*As long as the earth endures, seedtime and harvest, cold and heat, summer and winter, day and night will never cease.*" (NIV) The cycle of the seasons is one of those things that will never cease. After winter comes spring. It happens every year and it will continue without fail. Some winters are worse than others. Sometimes there are horrible snow storms or ice storms that prolong the winter, or for you folks up north there might be a late snow that prolongs the winter. We once received an Easter card from my aunt and uncle in Michigan saying it snowed the day they returned from spring break. That kind of thing may make it feel like winter is never going to end, but the fact of the matter is that spring always comes every year. The flowers always bloom, the birds always sing and the ground always thaws. The same is true for the seasons in your life. Your difficult circumstances won't last forever. It is a season. At times it may feel like there is no end to your misery, but I can assure you the spring will come and help is on the way.

Another thing you'll be able to see with your night vision goggles is that you are not alone. This is one of the biggest lies the enemy often tries to feed us: "Nobody else is going through this. Nobody else understands what I'm going through. Nobody cares about me and I'm in this by myself." Nothing could be further from the truth. This doesn't mean you don't feel like that. It just means how you feel may not be the truth of your circumstances. It is possible to isolate yourself from other people, but that is exactly the opposite of what you need when you are going through difficult circumstances. They may be difficult, but you need to ask for help. You need to engage others. Get in a small group and try and find others who are going through similar circumstances and can encourage you. One of the worst things you can do is have an ungrateful attitude and say, "Woe is me" while throwing a pity party for yourself. That's not to say what you are going through is not difficult and tremendously painful, but focusing on your pain will not help it go away, either.

It will help you to get around others in your church, small group or family that believe in Jesus and can encourage you in the Lord. My sister and her husband had a son a couple of years ago and the doctors thought he had a very rare disease called Reuben Stines Tabia, which is similar to Downs Syndrome. They are a great couple with great love for the Lord, and He has great plans for them. I can't tell you why this happened to them, but I can tell you that they are not alone. They belong to a great church, have great family support and have found comfort in those around them who have encouraged them. Best of all, they can take comfort in the Comforter himself. When Jesus was getting ready to physically leave His disciples, He told them *"and surely I am with you always, to the very end of the age"* (Matthew 28:20). (NIV) No matter how isolated or alone you may feel in your season of life, Jesus will be with you today, tomorrow, the next day, the day after that and the day after that. You get the point- every day.

The third thing you'll see with your night vision goggles is that there is hope. "*But we also rejoice in our sufferings, because we know that suffering produces perseverance; perseverance, character; and character, hope. And hope does not disappoint us*" (Romans 5:3b-5a). (NIV) No matter how difficult the season is you're going through, even in the season of death - there is always hope. Hope for tomorrow, hope for a new day, hope for eternal life. God explains in Psalm 30:5b that His mercies are new every morning for He says, "*Weeping may endure for a night, but joy comes in the morning*" (NKJV) Even in the worst of times there is hope each morning that His mercies will carry us through the day. Hope in God will not disappoint.

Sometimes when we have been pushed overboard and we're struggling to stay afloat, we are afraid to grab hold of the life preserver God throws us. We are afraid the rope will come loose and we'll be stuck floating in the ocean by ourselves. But when God throws us a life preserver, it is securely anchored to His son Jesus and it will not come loose no matter how hard we pull or no matter how high the waves get. The key is to keep hoping and hold on. There is something good and pleasant at the end of the rope – so hold on. Don't let go and don't give up hope.

In the story of Ruth, we see a young lady who held on to her mother in law, Naomi, in the hope of a new beginning. We don't hear about what happened to the other daughter in law, Orpah, but the Bible says that Ruth clung to her mother in law Naomi. Naomi's husband and two sons tragically died, so she decided to return home and try to find provision. She asked her two daughters-in-law to also return to their homes. But the Bible says that Ruth clung to Naomi. She was not going to let go, and she was not going to give up hope. So Ruth returned with Naomi and, lo and behold, Naomi found one of her relatives that was a suitable husband for Ruth. This man Boaz agreed to marry Ruth, and he restored honor back to Naomi and Ruth. Then to top it off, Boaz and Ruth had a son and they named him Obed. Obed was King David's Grandfather. There is always hope.

The last thing you will see with your night vision goggles is that the end is better than the beginning. It's the law of victory. No matter what round you're in, no matter how many times you have been knocked down, no matter how dizzy you are or how swollen your eyes may be from being pummeled, you are not down for the count. Not if Jesus is in your corner. You may be down, but you're not out. It didn't look good for Jesus when they crucified Him, speared Him and put Him in the grave, but three days later He rose from the dead. It may seem like the devil has the upper hand, but the Bible is very clear that he will be thrown into the lake of fire forever.

What better example of the law of victory could there be in contemporary history then the New Orleans Saints winning Super Bowl 44? The team that went 43 years without a NFC championship, much less a Super Bowl championship, the team that was known as the Aints, the team that had fans that wore paper bags over their heads, the team that almost left after Hurricane Katrina and almost quit when there were holes in her roof. But they didn't quit. They didn't give up. They continued on. They persevered. They kept the faith. They finished strong. And now, the team that wasn't, has become the team that is, and the Aints are the Saints and the Saints came marching home – Victoriously! The city of New Orleans, that suffered from the floods of the Hurricane, as the nation watched her agony of defeat and gasped at her despair, cheered and shook as the interception was returned and cherished her thrill of victory as the people filled her streets to welcome home her victors in the parade of

Saints. As her streets filled with people full of love and joy welcoming her conquering heroes, in the distance we heard her cry, redemption draweth nigh!

The victory of the Saints and of the City of New Orleans is but a foretaste of the feast that is to come for the saints of heaven will rise in victory at the call of the one who is, who was and who is to come. There will be no greater victory. There will be no larger parade. And the victory will be final. Every knee will bow and every tongue will confess that Jesus is Lord for He will reign forever and ever. No matter how bad it seems or how bad you feel, Jesus is the victor now and forever in your life. You may not be able to see it, but that' s why you need night vision goggles. You can' t see very clearly when it' s dark.

Put your night vision goggles on, read your Bible, go to a Bible believing church, get in a small group where you can get encouraged, and see beyond the darkness into the light that God has planned for you. When you' re looking into the darkness everything seems hopeless, but if you' ll look through your goggles you' ll see victory. You' ll see that we win. You' ll see that you' re not alone (Hebrews 13:5). You' ll see that there is hope. (Rom. 5:3) You' ll see that with God all things are possible (Philippians 4:13). You' ll see that if God is for you who can be against you (Romans 8:31). You' ll see that greater is He who is in you than he who is in the world (1 John 4:4). You' ll see that you are more than a conqueror (Romans 8:37). You' ll see that God has a great plan for your life and He' s not finished with you yet (Jeremiah 29:11).

Lord, help me to remember that though seasons come and go, You remain steadfast. Thank You for being the same yesterday, today and forever. Help me to see things through Your Son, Jesus Christ, and help me to be a light in the darkness. Thank You that Your mercies are new every morning. Amen.

Review & Begin Weekly Activity

Day 2: In Sickness And In Health

In the traditional wedding vows the phrase, "in sickness and in health" is exchanged between bride and groom. The implication is that no matter what condition your spouse is in physically, you will love and care for them.

Let me preface this discussion by saying that healing is the children's bread. The word of God is very clear that it is God's will for you to be healthy and whole. Your first response to sickness should always be to stand on God's promises and believe for His healing. *"He (Jesus) Himself took our infirmities and bore our sicknesses"* (Matthew 8:17). (NKJV) Jesus took stripes on His back so you could be healed *"But He was wounded for our transgressions, He was bruised for our iniquities; And by His stripes we are healed"* (Isaiah 53:5). (NKJV) But what do you do when the healing tarries? What do you do while you're waiting for your healing? What is your response when you have two children, and one is born with Down's syndrome and the other has been diagnosed as autistic? Hopefully as you wait on healing and strength, you can gain the ability to be thankful.

Are there any Biblical examples of God not healing? The Bible says that everywhere Jesus went He healed the sick, proclaimed the Good News and relieved the oppressed. But there is one example in 2 Corinthians 12 where Paul says he was given a thorn in the flesh. There has been a lot of controversy about what this thorn in the flesh was. It is not my intention to discuss what the thorn in the flesh was, but to demonstrate there was a thorn in the flesh that Paul couldn't get removed. I don't know what the thorn in the flesh was, but I do know a thorn in the flesh hurts, it's painful, and it can be disabling depending on where it's at. Most people have had encounters with thorns or thistles at one time or another and realize how painful they can be. But most of the time they just create some minor wounds that we clean and bandage and then we are on our way.

Paul, one of the greatest Apostles in the New Testament, had a thorn in the flesh that wouldn't go away. The Bible says he asked the Lord three times to take it away, but the Lord didn't. It's not easy to understand and even harder to try and explain, but one thing for sure is if this great apostle of the New Testament had something that wouldn't be healed, we should be careful not to judge others who are dealing with physical ailments, financial challenges or any other type of challenge that doesn't involve sin in their lives.

My wife and I had been in the New Orleans area for a year when Hurricane Katrina hit. We evacuated to Florida where Michelle's parents live. We arrived early Monday morning, and by Monday night had made the decision that I would return to see what help I could offer. I came back and worked with PRC Compassion in Gulf Port, MS for the next 6 weeks. The devastation alone was enough to steal my joy, but as if that was not enough, I blew a disk in my lower back while unloading a supply truck. At the time we did not have health insurance, and given that "normal" life had pretty much shut down in our area, going to a doctor was not an option. I knew I was where I needed to be, serving the victims, bringing some sort of hope to them, but the pain was very difficult. Honestly, because there was so much greater pain and suffering around me with all of the hurting people, I didn't think about it often. But after we returned to Louisiana, the pain continued. I slept on the floor, I sought relief through therapy, took Advil like it was candy and prayed continually for healing. It was hard for my children when I couldn't pick them up, and at times the pain was unbearable. After about two years God opened a door for me to have surgery, and my back has totally healed. I really can't explain why suffering happens. I can't tell you why bad things happen to good people, and I can't give you any reason for it other than because of this fallen world we live in. But there are some encouraging messages that God shares with us in His Word.

The first message comes from John chapter 9. The disciples were struggling with some of these very same questions. They saw a man born blind and *"His disciples asked him, 'Rabbi, who sinned, this man or his parents, that he was born blind?' 'Neither this man nor his parents sinned,' said Jesus, 'but this happened so that the work of God might be displayed in his life.' "* (NIV) There are some parents and there are some people that are struggling with illness that need to hear that again. It is neither this person nor his parents that sinned. It's not your fault. You didn't do anything wrong and you are not to blame for this illness.

The second encouraging message comes from Revelation 21:

"Behold, the tabernacle of God is among men, and He will dwell among them, and they shall be his people, and God Himself will be among them, and He will wipe away every tear from their eyes; and there will no longer be any death; there will no longer be any mourning, or crying, or pain; the first things have passed away." And He who sits on the throne said, "Behold, I am making all things new." (NASB)

As we said earlier we can't really explain some of our suffering in any way other than to say that we live in a sinful world. *It is an important reminder for us that this world is not our home.* We are citizens of heaven and in heaven, our true home, there will be no more tears and no more pain. God will make all things new. Take comfort in the fact that there will be a day when all of our disabilities and sicknesses will be wiped away forever.

I heard a story about a boy who came to his football coach one week and asked if he could start since he usually rode the bench. It was his senior year and the coach had second thoughts about it, but he decided to relent and let the boy start. The first play as the team kicked off, the boy ran down the field plowing through blockers and tackled the kick returner. The coach was stunned. On the first play from scrimmage, the boy broke through the line and tackled the quarterback. The coach was dumbfounded. The boy continued to play outstanding throughout the game, and when it finished he had 21 tackles, with 4 of them behind the line of scrimmage. The coach pulled him aside, told him that was the single best performance he had ever seen from one defensive player in a game, and asked him what happened? The boy replied, "My dad died this week and he was blind, so this is the first game that he got to watch me play from up in heaven." This world is not our home. We are citizens of heaven and when we get there, there won't be any more pain, suffering or disabilities.

The third message that God shares with us is in 2 Cor. 12:9b, *"My grace is sufficient for you."* (NKJV) Notice that God says it's **His** grace. It's not your grace or anybody else's grace, it's His grace. The same God who created you - the same God who knows everything about you - the same God who created the heavens and the earth, it's His grace. The same God who formed you in your mother's womb and the same God who knows how many hairs are on your head, it's His grace. Another thing is that God gives you His **grace** when there is something we can't understand. Grace is unmerited, undeserved and all encompassing. It is the mercy of God wrapped in a bow and presented to you as a gift. It is the gift of knowing that His ways are higher than our ways. Then the statement says that it **is** sufficient for you. Not maybe it will be sufficient, not it could be sufficient if such and such. It **is** sufficient—period. Then God communicates that it's **sufficient**. It's enough – nothing is lacking and there isn't anything missing or incomplete. God's grace is sufficient. Finally, God says that it's for **you**. It's not just for your neighbor or your children or your pastor or for anyone else, it's for you. God's grace is sufficient for you!

Paul says that God's power is made perfect in weakness, so he will boast about his weaknesses so that the power of Christ may dwell in him (2 Corinthians 12:9). Paul knew that when he was weak in the body, if he accepted God's grace for him, then he was made strong in Christ. That is why he was able to say that when he is weak, he is really strong. He meant that when he was weak in his body and relied on God and his grace, then he became strong in the Lord. The power of God would give him the strength to endure, overcome and even perform miracles, all because he recognized his own weakness and God's strength. The weaker I am, the stronger God needs to be and will be if I will believe that His grace is sufficient for me. Everything doesn't need to be perfect for me to believe that God will work in my life and the lives of those I minister to. In fact, God is more likely to work if I realize I am weak and don't have it altogether. That's okay because He does have it altogether. That way God gets all the glory. It's not me, it's Him. It's not my perfect prayer. God use my stammering tongue. It's not my great intelligence. God use my simple mind. It's not my great physical stature. God use my weak frame. It's not my great natural gifting. God use your Holy Spirit. Your power combined with anything of mine is still your power. Thank you for your grace – it is sufficient for me.

As we wait with God's strength and grace sustaining us, we must still remind ourselves of His promises. God's will is for you to be healthy and whole. He wants you to prosper and be in health. So while you're waiting, don't give up. Don't relinquish your hope. Don't stop believing. There may be times when you just need to rest and receive His grace, but you can't stay there. You have to keep trusting, keep believing and keep asking. Always remember, it's not your fault, heaven is your home and God's grace is sufficient for you. Never give up hope. Accept the hand that's been dealt to you, but see God's greater plans for your life. Keep praying.

I remember a time when I was believing God for a miracle in our finances. I had the privilege of occasionally working with mentally challenged individuals who folded boxes at the pizza place where I worked. I was talking to one young lady one day and was telling her how much Jesus loved her. At one point in our discussion she said "Jesus is not deaf." My response was "you mean Jesus is not dead. You're right, Jesus is not dead." Her immediate comeback to me was "No, Jesus is not deaf." What she didn't know was that just that week someone had sent us a check to pay off our consumer debt. I knew then that her words were sent by God to encourage me, to tell me He is listening to my prayers and to keep the faith. He had heard my prayers and He didn't forget about me. He won't forget about you, either. God is not deaf.

When we remember these messages from God, we find ways to be thankful even if our current condition is less than perfect health. We can be thankful when we understand that it's not our fault, heaven will wipe away all suffering and God's grace is sufficient for us. We can be thankful when we understand that God is more concerned about the health of our souls than the perfection of our body and as it says in 2 Corinthians 4 our suffering in this life is producing an eternal glory.

> *"Therefore we do not lose heart. Though outwardly we are wasting away, yet inwardly we are being renewed day by day. For our light and momentary troubles are achieving for us an eternal glory that far outweighs them all. So we fix our eyes not on what is seen, but on what is unseen. For what is seen is temporary, but what is unseen is eternal"* (2 Corinthians 4:16-18). (NIV)

We can be thankful for the parts of our body that are working. We can be thankful for the health that we have had, and the health that we are going to have. We can be thankful for the good moments, days and years. If you can't find anything else to be thankful for with regard to your health, try holding a mirror under your nose while your mouth is closed. If it fogs up, then you still got something!

Lord, I thank You that Your will for me is to be healthy and whole. However, if I face challenges with regard to my health, give me the strength to stand in thankfulness for what I do have, and to stand in faith believing for my healing whenever it is to come. Despite my physical weaknesses use my body Lord, to do Your work so You get all the glory!

Day 3: For Richer- For Poorer

When I said my wedding vows, I was honestly hoping for a lot more richer than I was poorer. Actually, I probably wasn't thinking about anything other than kissing the bride, but everyone wants more richer than poorer. Unfortunately, my wife and I have gone through some pretty intense times of "poorer," and we probably know a bit more about being thankful in this season than we would care to admit.

Although none of us know what lies ahead, as Christians we know that God has good things in store for us and that He wants to bless and prosper us, He says so in His word. *"Beloved, I pray that you may prosper in all things and be in health, just as your soul prospers"* (3 John 2). (NKJV) *"The wealth of the sinner is stored up for the righteous"* (Proverbs 13:22b). (NKJV) *"He who trusts in the Lord will be prospered"* (Proverbs 28:25b). (NKJV) God wants to meet your needs but even more than that He wants you to prosper. At the same time we need to remember that God wants us to be rich in good works more than He wants us to be rich in our bank accounts. What good will it do for us to gain the whole world and yet forfeit our souls?

One of the things we need to remember about prosperity is that it is a privilege and not a right. As a child of the King, I know that I am blessed and highly favored and I expect to prosper and have favor because my dad is the King. But prosperity is a privilege that I enjoy, not a right that I am entitled to. If I don't get what I want, or think that I deserve, I won't become embittered or ungrateful. The Lord owns the cattle on a thousand hills and all riches and honor are in His hand (Psalm 50:10). They are His cattle, His hills, and it's all in His hands. If He shares it with His son then I am indeed blessed, but if I don't prosper relative to others, then who am I to question the king? Unfortunately, our focus has become skewed due to our relative prosperity compared to the early church. In the early church they weren't praying for prosperity they were preaching the name of Jesus, praying for miracles and trying to avoid being killed. Jesus, knowing what his disciples would face, told them, "But s*eek first the kingdom of God and His righteousness and all these things shall be added unto you.*" (Matthew 6:33) (NKJV) Unfortunately, in many cases our goal has become prosperity instead of the kingdom of God.

So where does that leave you when you're believing God for increase, provision and blessing, but you're still living pay check to pay check? The first and foremost thing to remember is that God still loves you. You haven't necessarily done anything wrong that is blocking your blessing or ignored some financial principal of the kingdom that would unlock the gates of heaven. In fact, I think we have had enough seminars and presentations for a lifetime on how to get rich, or how to be a millionaire, or how to make $10,000 a month while working from home.

Rolling in the dough, or not, reflects neither positively nor negatively your relationship with God. There are a ton of rich people that are not even in relationship with God, and there are many more people struggling financially that are closer to God then we may ever know. Financial status is not an indicator of spirituality. Unfortunately, it has become all too common to think that the more money or blessing that someone has, the closer their relationship to God. Yes, every blessing comes from God, but just as the rain falls on the just and the unjust, so does wealth. Character is the true test of godliness. Godliness with contentment brings great gain. *Charm is deceitful and beauty is passing, but a woman who fears the Lord, she shall be praised* (Proverbs 31:30). (NKJV) Looking good, having nice things and being rich are all worldly and temporary. *"For bodily exercise profits a little, but godliness is profitable for all things, having promise of the life that now is and of that which is to come"* (1 Timothy 4:8). (NKJV)

Please don't misunderstand what I am saying. We should be good stewards of our finances and of our bodies - they are the temple of the Holy Spirit. And there is great blessing and abundance for God's children. If you are a child of the King, the King has a lot He wants to share with you. There is a reason why the patriarchs in the Old Testament were blessed abundantly. It is because God was their Father and He wants His kids to enjoy His blessings. But when we start to judge people's spirituality by the size of their pocketbooks, or their looks in the mirror, or by the size of their ministry, or success, then we end up with failure, corruption and sin just like in the world. Our values are different. What does your relationship with God look like? How do you treat people? How is your relationship with your spouse and your children? How is your personal integrity and character? Nobody is perfect, but these are the questions and the concerns of the church.

The church that I attend has a tremendous pastoral staff with great men of integrity that have great families. It is also a very blessed church financially and has had great growth. But the reason my wife and I go there isn't because it's a great mega church with lots of great amenities. Those are all just "extras." We go there because the Spirit of God is in the church, Jesus is preached, and people are being saved and discipled to be like Christ. It is the pastors, their relationships with God and their families that provide such a life giving environment for God's work to be accomplished, not the money. So please don't take one extreme and think that just because a church is big, blessed and growing that they must be doing something wrong just to attract people, or take the other extreme and think that just because a church is small and not financially booming there is something amiss.

Again, where does that leave you when you're believing God for increase and provision but you're still living check to check? You shouldn't be down on yourself or others because of your financial condition. God's expectation of you is not that you be rich, but that you are a good steward of what you have. Are you being a good steward? That is God's question no matter how much money you have. In fact, I think that you could make the argument that is easier to be a good steward with less money than more money. That's a good thing, because God's word tells us when we're faithful with the little that is when He will entrust us with more. "*Whoever can be trusted with very little can also be trusted with much, and whoever is dishonest with very little will also be dishonest with much*" (Luke 16:10). (NIV)

First, keep the big picture in mind. The big picture is like taking a snap shot with a camera so you can remember the overarching principles and promises of God. There are certain principles and promises in God's word that may not be evident in your immediate circumstances but they are still in the picture. The first one is stewardship. Just because you may be living check to check doesn't mean you aren't being a good steward, or that you're doing something wrong. It may be what you're doing right. Because we don't live in an agrarian society anymore, it is so hard for us to understand the concept of waiting for the harvest. It is so foreign to think about sowing seeds and waiting weeks, months, years or even generations to see the fruit of our labor. Think about the bamboo tree. It takes years of care and watering with very little signs of growth and then in one year it will grow eight times its size seemingly overnight. It won't ever hit its growth spurt if there aren't years of caretaking and watering. Remember to be faithful with whatever you have.

Another overarching principle in God's word is the blessing. God wants His children to be blessed. Keep His word and His promises in your heart. Don't give up believing. Don't give up faith. Even more than providing for your needs God wants you to prosper. You are His beloved child. He wants you to live in abundance so that you can help others. *"And God is able to make all grace abound to you, so that always having all sufficiency in everything, you may have an abundance for every good deed"* (2 Cor. 9:8). (NASB) He wants you to be blessed so that you can be a blessing. You are the head and not the tail. God wants you to have dominion on the earth. God created His sons and daughters to rule and reign in every sector of society. God created you for success and for victory. *" 'For I know the plans I have for you,' declares the Lord, 'plans to prosper you and not to harm you, plans to give you hope and a future' "* (Jer. 29:11). (NIV) So even if you don't see it in the natural continue to believe, confess and press into God's good plans for you as you wait on the harvest.

Just as we need to see the big picture so we can understand the concept of waiting for the harvest, we need to have an accurate perspective of the here and now. We need to zoom in so to speak and see how to apply the Word of God to our everyday lives. One perspective we see from the Bible is that God says He will provide for our needs. Philippians 4:19 says, *"And my God will supply all your needs according to His riches in glory in Christ Jesus."* (NASB) God is very clear that you as His child have the promise of having your needs met. You can come boldly before His throne in times of need. As the psalmist David said, "*Yet I have not seen the righteous forsaken, nor his descendants begging bread*" (Psalm 37:25b). (NKJV) Financial difficulty may affect us all, but if you are a child of the King He will meet your needs. "*Do not worry then, saying, 'What will we eat?' or 'What will we drink?' or 'What will we wear for clothing?' For the Gentiles eagerly seek all these things; for your heavenly Father knows that you need all these things. So do not worry about tomorrow; for tomorrow will care for itself.*" (Matt. 6:31-32,34a). (NASB)

Another perspective that we need to zoom in on is that we are all to run our own race. We each have unique and separate circumstances and differing conditions. No two people have the exact same family, faith, values, education, beliefs and influences in their lives. We each have our own race to run, mountains to climb and obstacles to avoid. "*Do you not know that those who run in a race all run, but only one receives the prize? Run in such a way that you may win*" (1Cor. 9:24). (NASB) Each of us is to run our race the way that God wants us to by being a good steward, believing His word, giving Him our first and best and caring for others. Then we will understand the meaning of true riches and that prosperity in God's economy applies to so much more than just money. It includes health, children, relationships, rest, favor, promotion, protection, peace and joy to name a few. So when God says that the blessing of the Lord makes one rich and He adds no sorrow with it, we need to understand that there is a richness that God provides other than finances alone. May you be released from the bondage of success in the world's eyes, and into success in God's eyes.

How else can we be thankful in difficult times? We can remember how rich we really are. In Chuck Bentley's <u>Crown</u>

Financial Radio Program, he shared the results of a poll indicating that about 7.6% of Americans have 8 million dollars. The astonishing thing was that of those polled, 2/3 considered themselves to be middle class and indicated they would need 13 million to be rich, and 24 million to be wealthy. We may not all have 8 million dollars, but when compared to the rest of the world, there is no one with a home in America that isn' t rich. We take our vacations, talk on our cell phones, go out to eat and drive one of our two cars to go pick up the kids from swim club, and think we have no money. I know I' ve done it. It' s because we are comparing ourselves with the car beside us, or the neighborhood down the street, instead of realizing that 3 billion people in the world live on less than $2 a day/ $60 a month; 1.6 billion live with no electricity or clean water, and 26,500 children die every day due to poverty, hunger and easily preventable diseases. You really *are* rich.

In conjunction with remembering how rich we really are, it is also helpful to assist others that are less fortunate. No matter how destitute you may feel, there are always others that have it worse, and it really puts things in perspective when you help those people. I know of one family that helps kids at a children' s home every Christmas to help them remember how much they have. They usually open up all their presents then they each pick one present to give to one of the kids. It' s probably more for the family than it is for the kids in the home, because they can see how blessed they are and keep everything in perspective.

Another way to be thankful in difficult circumstances is to give thanks for the little things, and be grateful for what you already have instead of worrying about what you don' t have. That' s what Jesus did when He found himself with a great need but little resources. He had a whole crowd of people to feed and His resources were limited to only five loaves of bread and two fish. *"Taking the five loaves and the two fish and looking up to heaven, He gave thanks and broke them. Then He gave them to the disciples to set before the people"* (Luke 9:16). (NIV) It's so easy to read over and miss – looking up to heaven He broke the bread and **gave thanks**. When Jesus took the little that He had and gave thanks for it, God miraculously multiplied it. I believe that God will do the same for you when you are in need. Not that we give thanks so that God will provide for us, but when our attitude is right and we thank God for what we have, we put ourselves in position to receive from God and see His miraculous provision. Think about how different this is than trying to beg, manipulate or depend on the government to meet our needs. That is not to say we don't need government assistance or help in times of need, but the focus is entirely different. One focuses on the need and demanding our rights, and the other on thanking God for what we have and depending on Him.

At the beginning of this section we talked about how God wants to bless us, and that He promises good for our lives. As we grow in our relationship with God, we may need to make adjustments regarding finances. We've already talked about the overarching principle of good stewardship. God has certain expectations set forth in His word for handling all of these blessings He bestows upon us. I know that the concept of tithing is controversial for some, but it is really the principle of giving God our first and our best. His expectation over and over in scripture is that we give Him our best and that we give to Him first - those are the gifts that are pleasing in His sight, not the ones that we throw in as tips from what's leftover. As far as additional offerings and giving is concerned, God is more concerned about the heart of the giver than with the gift. If your brother has something against you, go and make amends first

(Matthew 5:24). Then make your offering and God will accept it. God loves a cheerful giver and it's your attitude with your gift that makes it pleasing in God's sight. God also makes it clear that there are certain promises attached to our tithing and giving, but these principles of giving should not be our motive, simply the result. So as you thank God for your finances, make whatever adjustments you need to make. Save more, spend less, get out of debt, give God your first and best and give with a cheerful and thankful heart. Then the blessing of the Lord will make you rich and their will be no sorrow with it.

When I lost my job because I wasn't thankful for the money that I was making, within weeks of losing my job I had back surgery which left me unable to work for 2 months. Once I finally found stable work, we were already behind on bills. As we began to finally catch up, Michelle ended up having emergency surgery because of an ectopic pregnancy. This forced her to be out of work for two months. In addition, before all of this happened we thought we "needed" to buy a home, so we overextended ourselves and had a mortgage payment that was impossible to pay after I lost my job. Before long we found ourselves in serious financial trouble.

Although we were in the position we were in because of unwise decisions, we knew God had always taken care of us in the past and always would. We cried out to God, asked for his forgiveness for the ungrateful attitudes we'd had, and for the careless decisions we had made. Then we daily stood on His promises to give us what we needed. God in His amazing mercy showered us with blessings upon blessings upon blessings. He not only provided our immediate need for the daily necessities of food and shelter, but He provided us with things that we "wanted", but were not immediate needs. We ended up losing the house but gaining so much more. Because money was so tight, we told our kids Christmas would be very light this year. The youth group of a local church decided to adopt our kids for Christmas and showed up one Saturday with gifts for all of them. In addition, a complete stranger from the police department showed up on our door step and gave us $400 cash that he said was to be used for Christmas presents. My friends, God will provide for your needs and so much more. Be thankful for what you have, stand on His promises and trust Him to provide. He is so faithful.

Lord, thank You for giving me all that I have. Help me to be a good steward of what You have entrusted to me and to be content with what I have. Forgive me for the times I've complained about needing more. Guide me daily, Lord, and help me to seek Your face and not Your hand.

Day 4: For Better And For Worse

Many people feel like this has been one of the most perilous times in our country's history, with a slumping economy, corporate bankruptcies, declining housing markets, disease, natural disasters and terrorism all looming in the background. Many people have felt threatened, scared or trapped. But one of the ways we can alleviate these feelings and gain hope is by being thankful for the blessings and successes we are now experiencing, and by being thankful for our leaders, past and present, who have helped shape our country and ensure our freedom. Giving thanks and remembering what we have to be thankful for gives us hope for today and for our future.

One of the areas that a lot of people have concern about is with our current President, Barack Obama. I know that he is a very controversial figure for a lot of people, but I believe that if we can find a way as Christians to pray for and be thankful for him, God will bless our prayers and support and bring healing and reconciliation to our country. There is so much more on the line than how much you pay in taxes or how much money you have. I know there are a lot of concerns about his position on abortion, on civil unions and on Israel, but those are areas where he will be accountable to God some day, not to me. In fact, I am very thankful that we have a black president so that racial walls will be erased and that a greater understanding and unity will arise, especially in the church. I believe there will be a greater understanding between blacks and whites, and people will see that a black man can do as good a job or better than any white man, and that the job of white presidents in the past has not been as easy as it may have looked. One of the specific areas I am thankful for is that with a black president there will be many prejudices and stereotypes destroyed. In God's eyes, racism is just as grievous a sin as abortion because Jesus taught that hatred and anger are also considered murder (Matthew 5:21-22). As Christians, we need to lead in the area of racial reconciliation because we know that God is no respecter of persons. He doesn't see black, white, yellow or brown. God only sees red or not red, that is, either you are covered by the blood of Jesus or not. As far as our salvation is concerned, there are no other colors that God sees. In this respect you could say that God is color blind. Each of us will stand before God one day, and we will not give account for our color, race or nationality because these are determined by Him. We will have to give an account for what we have done with His Son Jesus.

Another thing that will bring us hope for today and the future is being thankful for the founding of our country. We can be thankful that our country was founded as one nation under God with liberty and justice for all. We can be thankful for our Christian heritage and the realization that all people are endowed by their Creator with certain unalienable rights. We can be thankful that the first act of America's Congress in 1774 was to ask a minister to open with prayer and to lead them in the reading of 4 chapters of the Bible. We can be thankful that in 1776 Congress approved the Declaration of Independence with 4 direct religious acknowledgements referring to God as the Creator, the Lawgiver, the Judge and the Protector. We can be thankful that the Liberty Bell was named for the Biblical inscription from Leviticus 25:10 which states, "Proclaim liberty throughout the land, to all the inhabitants thereof." We can be thankful that in 1777 Congress ordered 20,000 copies of the Bible to be imported to the States of the Union. We can be thankful that in 1789 Congress passed a law declaring that "religion, morality, and knowledge being necessary to good government and the happiness of mankind, schools and the means of education shall **forever** be encouraged."

We can be thankful that in 1789, on the same day that Congress finished drafting the First Amendment, it requested President Washington to declare a National day of prayer and thanksgiving, resulting in the first Federal official Thanksgiving proclamation that declared, "it is the duty of nations to acknowledge the providence of Almighty God, to obey His will, to be grateful for His benefits, and humbly to implore His protection and favor." We can be thankful that in 1870 the Federal Government made Christmas an official holiday, that it was declared by the U.S. Supreme Court that Christmas has been acknowledged in the Western World for 20 centuries, and in this country by the people, the Executive Branch, Congress, and the courts for 2 centuries.

We can give thanks for our current President and we can give thanks for our past presidents. None of them were perfect, but we can be thankful that Thomas Jefferson urged local governments to make land available specifically for Christian purposes, provided Federal funding for missionary work among Indian tribes, and declared that religious schools would receive 'the patronage of government'. We can be thankful that President Franklin D. Roosevelt not only led the Nation in a 6 minute prayer during D-Day on June 6, 1944, but he also declared that, "If we will not prepare to give all that we have and all that we are to preserve Christian civilization in our land, we shall go to destruction." We can be thankful that President Dwight D. Eisenhower declared, "Without God there could be no American form of government, nor an American way of life." We can be thankful that President John F.

Kennedy declared, "The rights of man come not from the generosity of the state but from the hand of God."

Considered by many the greatest president in our country's history, Abraham Lincoln said that the Bible "is the best gift God has given to men..... But for it, we could not know right from wrong." Lincoln was also responsible for adopting and signing a proclamation for a national day of prayer and fasting. Although the proclamation is lengthy, I think it so profound and weighty that it deserves to be included for your reading and reflection. The proclamation states:

> "And whereas it is the duty of nations as well as of men, to own their dependence upon the overruling power of God, to confess their sins and transgressions, in humble sorrow, yet with assured hope that genuine repentance will lead to mercy and pardon; and to recognize the sublime truth, announced in the Holy Scriptures and proven by all history, that those nations only are blessed whose God is the Lord.
>
> And, insomuch as we know that, by His divine law nations like individuals are subjected to punishments and chastisements in this world, may we not justly fear that the awful calamity of civil war, which now desolates the land, may be but a punishment, inflicted upon us, for our presumptuous sins, to the needful end of our national reformation as a whole People? We have been the recipients of the choicest bounties of Heaven. We have been preserved, these many years, in peace and prosperity. We have grown in numbers, wealth and power, as no other nation has ever grown. But we have forgotten God. We

have forgotten the gracious hand which preserved us in peace, and multiplied and enriched and strengthened us; and we have vainly imagined, in the deceitfulness of our hearts, that all these blessings were produced by some superior wisdom and virtue of our own. Intoxicated with unbroken success, we have become too self-sufficient to feel the necessity of redeeming and preserving grace, too proud to pray to the God that made us!

It behooves us then, to humble ourselves before the offended Power, to confess our national sins, and to pray for clemency and forgiveness."

This type of statement was not signed and adopted by a pastor or a church; it was signed and adopted by a President of our United States of America. As Americans, we possess a Christian heritage we should truly be thankful for. We often take this heritage for granted because it is not something we' ve earned, but as the word implies, we' ve inherited it. The blessings we now enjoy were earned by the selfless giving and sacrifice of our forefathers. That is why we need to be so thankful and not take for granted what was earned at such great cost. Otherwise, it is in danger of being lost.

Isaiah 54:17 says, " *'No weapon formed against you will prosper; And every tongue that accuses you in judgment you will condemn. This is the heritage of the servants of the Lord, and their vindication is from Me,' declares the Lord."* (NASB) As servants of the Lord, this is your heritage. If you are a servant of the Lord you can claim this truth of Scripture that no weapon formed against you will prosper, that every tongue that accuses you will be condemned and that you will be vindicated by the Lord. You can claim these promises as your own because of your heritage. Jesus was the ultimate servant of the Lord who lived a sinless and perfect life, and He is the one who earned the heritage of blessing that you now experience. It was Jesus' perfect life – His death and His resurrection- that earned you the heritage you have in the Lord. The promises God made to His Son are yours because of your belief and association with Jesus. Because of your belief in Jesus, the promises God made to Him are now your heritage.

A heritage is like an inheritance; it is given, not earned. This heritage has been inherited and received by no effort on your own, but through the work of Christ. We must believe in Him and His promises so we can participate in the heritage that has been earned for us. If we are not thankful for this work, and if we do not believe in the heritage that has been earned for us, then we can't experience the blessings that are attached to it. The same is true for the Christian heritage of our country. If we are not thankful for it and believe in it, we are in danger of losing the blessings attached to that costly heritage. If we are not thankful for our heritage, we are in effect rejecting our inheritance. Let us be thankful for our Christian heritage, and let us receive all of the blessings of the inheritance that have been earned by those who have sacrificially gone before us.

There are a multitude of reasons to be thankful if we will just take the time to remember what we have inherited from everyone that has gone before us, including presidents and soldiers. We need to be thankful for the blood that has been shed by every soldier, every limb that's been severed and every life that's been lost. Many, many soldiers have paid a great price for our freedom and for the rights and privileges we now possess, but we often take for granted: the freedom of speech; the freedom to vote; the freedom to assemble and worship our Lord and Savior Jesus Christ. These soldiers did not die in vain, and they did not die so we could have freedom *from* religion; they died so we could have the freedom *of* religion without government control or interference. Jesus died for our souls, but there are many soldiers that have died for our freedom. Give thanks to God for our freedom. Be thankful for our presidents, current and past, our history, our country and our heritage.

Dear Lord, these words of prayer are so important...not only for all of us in this country...but for the entire world! Yes, this special prayer is for our new President Barack Obama...the man who will be leading us in the years to come. Please, please be with him! Give him the wisdom to guide us through these rough, hard times. Show him the right ways to overcome the many terrible situations we are now facing. And grant him the strength to shoulder such heavy burdens day by day. Please keep President Obama safe under Your Wing, Dear Lord, and let him know in his heart that we are thankful for him...and that we are always remembering to pray for him and his family. Thank You, Lord, for hearing these words of special prayer that I now offer in Jesus' Name. Amen. (Life Study Fellowship, Noroton, Connecticut)

Lord, thank You for our country and the freedoms we have. I'm in awe of the sacrifices made by others to ensure my freedom here in America. Help me to always remember how blessed I am to live in the Land of the Free and the Home of the Brave. Thank You for the ultimate freedom You give me in Christ. Amen.

Day 5: In Laws And Out Laws

Thankfully, I don't really have any outlaws in my family. My in-laws are a real blessing to our family. I'm not just saying that to try and find something to be thankful for with regard to them. My wife's parents and my parents have always gotten along well and we have celebrated together, taken vacations together, etc. In fact, my in-laws might just get along too well with my parents because sometimes they gang up on us when they don't see us making decisions they think we should be making. This is a good challenge to have, however, because they love and care for us so much, and I can not express the gratitude for the love and assistance both our parents have given us.

I fully realize that some of you may not be as blessed as we have been with our families, and the mere mention of in-laws sends chills down your spine. Just the thought of talking about your in-laws gets you into an argument with your spouse. I understand this can be a real challenge. Even if it's a challenge, you can be thankful that they produced your spouse. If not, then we'll work on being thankful for your spouse on another day. The idea is that it doesn't matter how difficult your in-laws are or what your family background is. You can find a branch of your family to be thankful for.

When our second daughter, Maddy, prays at night, it is so sweet to hear how she prays quite frequently, "Thank you, Lord, for putting me in the perfect family." I'm not sure where she heard it or even when she started praying it, but it touches my heart every time she prays that. You may not be able to pray that prayer, but there is someone somewhere in your family lineage you can be thankful for. Maybe you have to go back a couple of generations, but there is someone. Someone who loved God, someone who prayed for their future descendants, someone who stayed faithful until the end and someone who did what was right and just. Even if you are the first Christian ever in your family, you can be thankful for your heritage and for God saving those eight people from the flood. Be thankful that Noah believed God.

Josiah was a great king in the Old Testament. His father, however, was wicked and his grandfather was one of the most wicked kings in the history of Judah. Josiah didn' t use that as an excuse to follow in their footsteps. Josiah made a decision that he was going to find someone in his family to be thankful for and follow in their footsteps. Josiah was thankful for David and skipped over generations of wickedness to be thankful for his great, great, great, great... grandfather. *"And he did what was right in the sight of the Lord, and walked in the ways of his father David; he did not turn aside to the right hand or to the left. For in the eighth year of his reign, while he was still young, he began to seek the God of his father David"* (2 Chronicles 34:2-3a). (NKJV) No matter what kind of family you were raised in and no matter how ungodly their examples might have been, there is a Righteous Branch you can be thankful for. Ultimately, our Righteous Branch is Jesus, who descended from King David (Jeremiah 23:5; 33:15). Josiah could have easily followed in the footsteps of his father or grandfather, but the Bible tells us that he walked in the ways of his father David.

God is so gracious and merciful that He can even place us into spiritual family who can fill voids left by blood family. One of the classic examples in Scripture is the story of David and Jonathon. David was many times forgotten by his father and despised by his brothers. Yet God gave him a great friend to confide in, a friend that was closer than a brother. 1 Samuel 18:1b says *"the soul of Jonathan was knit to the soul of David, and Jonathan loved him as his own soul."* (NKJV) Who has God placed in your life that you can be thankful for? They may not be related to you by blood, but rather by the blood of Christ. Maybe you grew up as an only child and you've got a great small group that seems better than brothers or sisters. Maybe you never had a good relationship with your father and God has placed a spiritual leader in your path to help you. Be mindful of those people today and thank God for them.

In November of 2007, my wife Michelle had an ectopic pregnancy. If that wasn't hard enough, our families live nowhere close to us, but we were extremely blessed that Michelle's mom was able to come help. My mom came as well, but because their coming meant securing flights and travel arrangements we had about a week where we had to deal with this alone. Praise God He placed us in the most amazing spiritual family. We went to the ER, knowing our three girls would be picked up from school and cared for by this spiritual family. We had Josiah with us, and while we were in the emergency room waiting for the plan of what we needed to do and where Josiah would stay, he got sick. For the next 10 days he had the stomach flu. I can't tell you the number of families that took turns watching our kids, including Josiah, knowing there was a good chance they would catch this stomach bug he had. They gave and gave and gave sacrificially, as if we were truly members of their family. Some of Michelle's closest friends cleaned our house, did our laundry and brought us meals. We had people from other churches bringing us food, simply because God united us together with them as spiritual family.

I know the statistics and I know how the family has disintegrated in society with divorce rates and single parents doing the best that they can. I also know that others of you have suffered great injustices of abuse, neglect, and a lack of love in your homes at the hands of people in your family. That is not God' s plan and He is not the author of that pain and abuse. Even if you still are having trouble finding a family to be thankful for, remember that God is love and He is the one who has provided a Righteous Branch for your family. He is the one who is calling to you and wanting to bring healing and hope to your areas of pain. God is true though every man be a liar. God is not trying to manipulate, trick or secretly hurt you. If you don' t have anyone else who truly loves you just the way you are, if you don' t know anyone else who cares about the pain you' ve endured, if you don' t have anyone else who understands what you' re going through, God does. God is not like us, He loves you just because. His love is unconditional.

He is the loving Father waiting for you to call upon Him so that He can help you in your time of need. He' s sitting on His throne just waiting for you to return home, and when He sees you coming He' ll jump up and run down the streets of gold just to sweep you up into His arms. Romans 8:16-17 tells us "....*we are children of God, and if children, then heirs*....." (NKJV) If you have nothing else to be thankful for, as a follower of Christ you are a part of God' s family.

There are young people reading this that may have felt betrayed by families who have divorced, used drugs and called them names; betrayed by families that have claimed to be Christian but did not care about Christ; betrayed by families that made you go to church on Christmas and Easter, but did not care about it on Monday or Tuesday. We have all seen the consequences of our country turning away from God. Increased violent crimes, shootings in schools, terrorist attacks on our own soil, and drug and sex trafficking. Even our church leaders and presidents have had public moral failures. We have experienced the type of world that has come from the "freedom" revolution. Although there was some good that came in the way of racial and gender equality, the damage done to the moral fiber of our society has caused such pain and heartache, that only by the grace of God can it be overcome.

God is raising up a righteous generation in His family that will serve Him in spirit and in truth; a generation that will restore the purposes of the academic institutions and the founding fathers; a generation that instead of flaunting freedom in the face of God, will restore righteousness and justice to the American way and use that freedom to serve God with all their hearts; a generation that will set the course of America closer to the direction that God intended it, unlike the generation of the 60's that moved it away from God's chartered course. Many have prayed for revival and reformation, but God's perfect timing has not been to use previous generations that have participated in this waywardness and contributed to the great turning away of America. God is raising up a new generation of people to possess the Promised Land, and to turn the tide of America back toward God where there will be no doubt that we are a Christian Nation Under God and no one will be able to question it. They may complain, they may move and they may try and retaliate, but they will not win. This nation was founded as a Christian Nation Under God and it is still and always will be. Just as the Israelites disobeyed God and turned away from Him, there was a period of wandering that took place in the desert and they were not allowed to enter into the Promised Land until a new generation arose. So now, there is a new generation that is rising up to take their place in our world that will follow God, possess the land and return our hearts to their Creator.

God is raising up a generation of Joshua's that are going to possess the land. Joshua stood before the people of Israel and unashamedly declared, *"As for me and my house we will serve the Lord"* (Joshua 24:15c). (NKJV)   Young people, dads, single moms rise up in your family. I don't care what has happened up until this point, I don't care about the past and I don't care about what may happen in the future, as for me and my household we will serve the Lord. God's encouragement to Joshua then and to you today is *"be strong and very courageous, that you may observe to do according to all the law which Moses My servant commanded you; do not turn from it to the right hand or to the left, that you may prosper wherever you go. This Book of the Law shall not depart from your mouth, but you shall meditate in it day and night, that you may observe to do according to all that is written in it. For then you will make your way prosperous, and then you will have good success. Have I not commanded you? Be strong and of good courage; do not be afraid, nor be dismayed, for the Lord your God is with you wherever you go"* (Joshua 1:7-9). (NKJV)

I remember after Hurricane Katrina that one of the positive elements from the storm that I kept hearing about was how the storm brought family and friends together. Storms and struggles have a funny way of doing that. Over and over again I heard about how eighteen people inconveniently crammed into a two bedroom house, but it brought their family closer together and they saw and bonded with family members they didn't even know that they had. It was a time to be thankful for family and friends and it was a time to forget personalities and annoying quirks and count on one another in a time of need. It was a time to get along with in laws and out laws and a time to put differences aside so that people could survive. It is during times like that when you learn to be thankful for your family.

No matter what your family tree looks like (with all the separations and divorces it may look more like a bush than a tree) God is with you wherever you go. Be strong and very courageous and do not turn to the right or to the left. Be thankful for whatever you can be thankful for in your family, and make the most of it by declaring, "as for me and my house we will serve the Lord." No matter what your past, no matter what your pain and no matter how dim your picture may look – you can make a change, you can break free, you can change history and you can chart a new path for your family. You can' t control your past but you can control the decisions you make today, and when you turn to the Lord you will find that His mercy endures forever and His faithfulness is from generation to generation. Make a choice today that as for you and your household, you will serve the Lord and become someone who others in future generations of your family will be thankful for.

Father God, thank You for being truly that to me, a Father. Thank You that by Your grace I have been adopted into Your family. Thank You for loving me unconditionally. Help me to impact those around me to expand Your family.

Amen

Day 6: It Was The Best Of Times, It Was The Worst Of Times

We have a saying in our family. I'm not really sure how it originated and it may have come from somewhere else, but it's a little rhyme that goes like this. "You get what you get, don't throw a fit" and, "You get what you get, be thankful for it." It's especially useful at dinner time when the kids look at their plates and say, "What is this? Ooough, that looks gross. I don't like this! What else can I have? I'm not hungry." It's also useful in curbing sibling rivalry when each of the kids get presents and there is a tendency to look at their sister's toy and want that one instead. They might be thinking it, but if they say it they're going to get a "You get what you get, be thankful for it." There are things they are praying for and hoping for, but contentment begins with being thankful for what you already have.

This week your assignment has been to make lists every day of what you're thankful for. I'm wondering if it has helped open up your eyes to the everyday blessings and miracles of life. I know when I start to think about what I'm thankful for, even the little things in my life take on great meaning. Every morning I usually pray and ask God to bless me. I don't just ask Him to bless me, I usually ask Him to bless me abundantly (don't worry He's got enough blessing for you, too). I remember reading Bruce Wilkinson's book _Beyond Jabez_, believing God for more blessing, and adding the idea that I wanted God to bless me the way _He_ wants to bless me. Instead of naming my desired blessings and determining whether God answered my prayer based on whether He did what I wanted or not, I was asking Him to bless me however *He* wanted. It was amazing to see His hand at work. From kind words, to unexpected finances and even better food than I anticipated, it was and is wonderful to see God's blessings in my life. When you give God control of your blessings, even the little things mean so much. I remember one day after believing God to bless me, I came home late from work and all three of my girls were sleeping in the same room and they were all awake in the middle of the night. I don't know how they all woke up at the same time, but I thank God that I got to say hi and give them all a kiss good night.

We must always remember that we have to be thankful for the manna that God provides us, even if it looks, feels and tastes differently than we expected. We aren't always going to experience the promised land blessings. There aren't always going to be warm fuzzy feelings in our bellies. There aren't always going to be trips to Disney World. We aren't always going to be able to eat out at our favorite restaurants. It's these times, when we are tempted to complain, "I'd rather this", or "I want that", that we need to stop and thank God for the little things. Often times it's the little things that God provides that we overlook. I remember realizing this when I was working for tips.   I needed to be thankful for the little tips as well as the big ones. It was very easy for me to praise God for the big tips and just as easy to complain when I didn't get any tips at all. However, God was providing and I needed to be thankful for even the littlest tips. There was a time when I was fasting from meats and desserts, and our family was in great financial distress after my back surgery. A friend of mine gave us about 50 hamburgers from an outreach event he held. Instead of tossing out the burgers, I decided to be thankful for what God provided and only eat the burgers instead of eating no meat. I hope that God didn't mind. Manna looks so good when you're in the desert, but by the end of the burgers I was starting to relate with the Israelites who complained about their manna. No matter what our circumstances, we have got to find a way to be thankful for the little things.

One of the things we need to realize is that it could always be worse. If you were dead, it couldn't be any worse because you'd be in Heaven. But then you wouldn't be reading this, would you? We need to focus on being thankful for our blessings while we have them. We need a greater appreciation and a greater sense of how good we really do have it. God is so good. He has blessed me so much. Even this computer that I am typing on was a gift from God that came just at the perfect time, so that I could spend more time working on this book. I am so thankful for our family room furniture, for our TV and DVD player, for my golf clubs and my bed, for all my work shirts and for an iron that works, and for the food in our cupboards. As my Grandma Beach would say – Thank you Jesus!

We have to find a way to smell the roses, even if we prefer tulips; to be thankful for the sun in the sky, even when we don't have sunglasses; to be thankful for the rain that makes the flowers grow, even when it's raining on our parade; to be thankful for the fragrance of spring, even if it triggers our allergies; to be thankful for the harvest of the summers, even if we do live in Louisiana where it's 110 degrees. We need to find a way to be thankful for the blessings in our lives that we take for granted every day. Clean drinking water, hot showers, good tasting food and every breath that we take. Recently, before trading in our old van for a newer one, we had everyone in our family go around and share about what they were thankful for about the old van. We talked about the fun trips we had taken, about God keeping us safe in it, about the songs we had sung in it, and about the fact that we never had a blown tire while driving etc, etc. Of course, then there was a little separation anxiety with the kids when we left the old van and took the new one, but I looked at it as a good thing because they were thankful and grateful for the old one. We have to find a way to be thankful in everything. For Christmas one year, I got a belt that was fine, but I wasn't that excited about it so I was really thinking about how I could be thankful for it. I figured I could use it for work and be thankful for it because I wouldn't have to wear my "good" belt to work and ruin it. Now I wear it with thankfulness.

You can really apply this to anything you have. Right now in the house that we're renting, we have a stove that doesn't heat above 350. Is it inconvenient and would we like it fixed? Yes, but we are thankful that it works at all. If you don't have an oven then be thankful for your microwave, and if you don't have a microwave be thankful for fire – you get the picture. Find something that you can be thankful for and focus on that instead of what's wrong, what's missing or what's broken. The worst thing we can do is focus on all the problems we have or the problems that something we own has. That is only going to cause us to be ungrateful. But if we'll be thankful for even the little things that are right with what we have, then we'll find we're being thankful in everything.

In addition to giving us some great examples to follow in the Bible – God also gave us some great examples of what *not* to do. 1 Corinthians 10:6-11 says, "*Now these things became our examples, to the intent that we should not lust after evil things as they also lusted. And do not become idolaters as were some of them. As it is written, 'The people sat down to eat and drink, and rose up to play.' Nor let us commit sexual immorality, as some of them did, and in one day twenty three thousand fell; nor let us tempt Christ, as some of them also tempted, and were destroyed by serpents; nor* complain, as some of them also complained, and were destroyed by the destroyer. Now all these things happened to them as examples, and they were written for our admonition, upon whom the ends of the ages have come." (NKJV) I don't know about you, but I don't want to be destroyed by the destroyer. I need to be careful not to complain about my food, my circumstances, my possessions or my spiritual leaders. I want God's blessing, not destruction.

I'm not that good at it all the time - that's why I'm practicing Thankability, but I got this story in an email from a friend that explains perfectly our choice to choose our attitude. "*When I was a kid, my mom liked to make breakfast food for dinner every now and then. And I remember one night in particular when she had made breakfast after a long, hard day at work. On that evening so long ago, my mom placed a plate of eggs, sausage and extremely burned biscuits in front of my dad. I remember waiting to see if anyone noticed! Yet all my dad did was reach for his biscuit, smile at my mom and ask me how my day was at school. I don't remember what I told him that night, but I do remember watching him smear butter and jelly on that biscuit and eat every bite! When I got up from the table that evening, I remember hearing my mom apologize to my dad for burning the biscuits. And I'll never forget what he said:*

'Honey, I love burned biscuits.' Later that night, I went to kiss Daddy good night and I asked him if he really liked his biscuits burned. He wrapped me in his arms and said, 'Your Momma put in a hard day at work today and she's real tired. And besides - a little burnt biscuit never hurt anyone!'"

So much of our happiness and contentment – and ultimately our thankfulness – is determined by our attitude. We have a choice- every day – to look at what we have and be truly thankful, or to grumble and complain. Deuteronomy 11:26 in the New Living

Translation says *"Look, today I am giving you the choice between a blessing and a curse."* God gives us the choice, we can choose for ourselves a life full of blessing – even if it's the things we think of as "normal" like running water, or we can choose for ourselves a life full of complaining and cursing. We can speak life into our situations with our thankfulness, or we can speak cursing into our life with our grumbling. James warns of this in chapter 3 of his epistle. *"From the same mouth come both blessing and cursing. My brethren, these things ought not to be this way"* (James 3:10).(NASB)

John Kilpatrick tells a powerful story about when he realized how much his ungrateful attitude affected the blessings God had for him. Their new church contained an orchestra pit. Pastor Kilpatrick tells how he quickly became less than excited about this orchestra pit when no one seemed interested in playing in an orchestra. Rather than thank God for this orchestra pit, he began to grumble and complain about it. God dealt with him about his attitude and told him to stop cursing it. Soon after he began blessing the orchestra pit and being thankful for it, the pit was filled will all kinds of musicians and instruments, so much that they had to turn people away.

God did not promise us life on this earth would be full of brand new cars, sirloin steaks and perfect relationships all the time. Continue to take the time at the end of each day and reflect on what you have to be thankful for, even if it's not the best of everything that life has to offer. Stop throughout your day and look for the small miracles that happened. It's easy to see and be thankful for the miracles of healing in cancer patients. But today, how about thanking God for the miracle of a child sleeping soundly for a two hour nap while you were able to get a few things done? Or how about the miracle of the telephone that allowed you to call a friend and share a laugh? How about the miracle of living in a country where there's a store on almost every corner where you can buy milk? We can truly live a life full of blessing if we have the right attitude.

Lord, thank You for my home – the house I live in and the amazing family I live with. Thank You that I have food every day. Thank You that I have a car to drive and feet to carry me where I need to go. Thank You for the grass and flowers around my home that add color to my day. Thank You for the stop lights that add safety to my travels. Thank You for the frogs and crickets that lull me to sleep at night. Thank You for blessing me with life, life made more abundant through You. Amen.

Complete & Reflect On Weekly Activity

GIVING THANKS IN ADVERSITY

Day 1: Introduction & Keep Your Eyes On The Prize

The whole concept of adversity is very painful for some people to even think or read about. It is not something we look forward to or desire, yet it is still part of this fallen world and a reality in our lives. Jesus said in this world you will experience trouble, but do not fear because He has overcome the world (John 16:33). My hope this week as we deal with being thankful, even in the midst of adversity, is that we come to a new level of thanksgiving and see God's hand of providence, even in the midst of our pain. I pray that we can see beyond the pain and suffering of this world to the unseen protection and blessing of God. I hope that as we explore this theme of adversity and see the examples that have been set before us from our great fathers and mothers in the faith, that we will find new hope and strength to endure the pain of this life. When adversity comes may we be *"afflicted in every way, but not crushed; perplexed, but not despairing; persecuted, but not forsaken; struck down, but not destroyed"* (2 Corinthians 4:8-9). (NASB)

I do not want to minimize any adversity or loss you are going through or have been through. Believe me, I know what it's like to go through tough times. I've lost my job. I've lost my house. I've lost a child due to miscarriage. I've had health challenges. I've had a rocky marriage. I hope that at the very least, you will find comfort and healing in relating with others who have experienced pain and loss but continued to be faithful to God. Even in the most severe adversity of losing a loved one or even a child, you have a God who sees your tears and who willingly gave up His Son for your life.

So come Holy Spirit, bind up the broken hearted, heal the sick, set the captives free and proclaim the favorable year of the Lord. (Isaiah 61)

One of the things my pastor has emphasized about facing adversity is that we don't see a command to give thanks *for* adversities. It is a command to give thanks *in* adversity. Paul says in I Thessalonians 5:18, "*in everything give thanks.*" In Paul's letter to the Thessalonians, he challenges them to persevere despite their persecution and is clear that throughout this persecution they are to continue giving thanks. Even Jesus wasn't thankful **for** suffering the cross, He was thankful **even though** He was suffering the cross. Think of the Garden of Gethsemane. Jesus didn't go there saying, "Thank you for this opportunity to suffer." Jesus said, "Please take this cup from me, but not my will, but your will be done." Thank you, God.

There is just a slight difference in words, but it is the difference between an unrealistic and unwarranted attitude that says, "Lord, thank you for this suffering – give me more" and the Biblical model that says, "Lord, I thank you even though I'm going through this horrible adversity; I trust you and I know you're going to work good out of this situation." Obviously, as we learn how to be thankful in every circumstance, this is one of the most challenging times to be thankful. But it is also one of the best times to enter into a focused and directed time of thanksgiving and praise. When we trust in God and say, "Lord, I'm in pain and I'm hurting because of...," but we find a way to be thankful in the midst of these circumstances, that is when we find God's sufficient grace and discover He is always there for us in our time of need. One of the encouragements I would give you is that God is big enough to handle your questions and your doubts. Bring them without blaming Him, with a heart of thanksgiving, and you will taste and see that the Lord is good.

In week 2 we made lists of everything we were thankful for. Now in week 3, what I am asking you to do is go deeper with your lists of thanksgiving. Your assignment this week is to keep a journal each day telling God *why* you' re thankful or *how* you' re feeling or maybe even why you' re struggling to be thankful.

In a research project on gratitude and thankfulness, Emmons and Michael McCullough from the University of California and the University of Miami discovered the following benefits of keeping such a gratitude journal (www.darwinismrefuted.com).

- In an experimental comparison, those who kept gratitude journals on a weekly basis exercised more regularly, reported fewer physical symptoms, felt better about their lives as a whole, and were more optimistic about the upcoming week compared to those who recorded hassles or neutral life events (Emmons & McCullough, 2003).

- A related benefit was observed in the realm of personal goal attainment: Participants who kept gratitude lists were more likely to have made progress toward important personal goals (academic, interpersonal and health-based) over a two-month period compared to subjects in the other experimental conditions.

- Participants in the daily gratitude condition were more likely to report having helped someone with a personal problem or having offered emotional support to another, relative to the social comparison condition.

- In a sample of adults with neuromuscular disease, a 21-day gratitude intervention resulted in greater amounts of high energy positive moods, a greater sense of feeling connected to others, more optimistic ratings of one's life, and better sleep duration and sleep quality, relative to a control group.

- Children who practice grateful thinking have more positive attitudes toward school and their families (Froh, Sefick, & Emmons, 2008).

So get writing. Be honest. This is for your benefit, and it is an act of faith to release the power of God into your circumstances and heal wounds and brokenness from adversity that you've experienced. Men, this is not just an exercise for the women. Although they may be more inclined to share their feelings and keep a journal, it is only for a week and you don't have to get up and share this in your small group. It is between you and God and He would love to hear about how you're really feeling. (He already knows, but He wants you to talk to Him.) My hope as you share your heart and feelings with God is that He will pour out his goodness and mercy on you, and that He will help you to become even more thankful than you already are.

Keep Your Eyes On The Prize

With the times that we are living in it is easy to understand that adversity will come. It is not a personal phenomenon that only some people have tough times. As we grow closer to the time when Jesus returns we are experiencing more and more birth pains corporately as a people, a nation and a world. But this does not have to affect the attitude that we live with on a daily basis. At the same time, it is quite true that we are living in the end times and that we have been experiencing heartache, pain and adversity, whether it has been the financial crisis, the hurricane force winds, the purifying fires or the earthquakes of adversity. The question then is not whether these times will come into our lives, for time and chance happen to them all, but how we will respond when these events happen.

As I thought about the Biblical examples of adversity, one of the stories that resonated in my mind was the story of Jacob. I think part of the reason that his circumstances seem so painful to me is because of our fast paced, fast food, microwave society. When I read and think about Jacob's story in Genesis 29-31, I am amazed at the patience, determination and focus that Jacob maintained through all that he went through. For those of you not familiar with the story – Jacob is sent by his parents to a place called Paddan Aram to find a wife so that he won't marry a Canaanite woman. When he arrives he becomes completely enamored with a girl named Rachel who is part of Jacob's mother's family and evidently suitable in those times for marriage. So Jacob goes to meet Rachel's father. You know the big meeting of the in-laws for the very first time and he is introduced to his Uncle Laban. Evidently there were no shotguns involved and the meeting went well so Jacob begins to work for his father – in-law. After about a month, Laban asks Jacob what he would like to be paid and because Jacob is so in love with Rachel he offers to work seven years for the hand in marriage of his daughter. Laban agrees and Jacob begins his seven years of hard labor (see Genesis 31:40). The Bible says something very interesting that boggles my mind. It says that Jacob served seven years to get Rachel, but they seemed like only a few days to him because of his love for her. Wow! Talk about focus. This man was unbelievable. He went through long hours, sleepless nights, heat by day and cool by night and it only felt like a few days. How is that possible?

Jacob kept his eyes on the prize. Talk about discipline, talk about focus, talk about an example for young people today who burn with passion for one another who can hardly wait for an hour much less seven years. This is unheard of and it points to Jacob's thankful heart that didn't focus on the work and adversity that he endured, but instead he kept his eye on the prize and his adversity and work only seemed like a few days to him. Believe me he knew the pain, the heartache and the long hours that filled his life, but when he laid his head down at night his focus was not on resentment and adversity, it was on the love of his life and the time flew by for him.

I wish I could say that Jacob's adversity ended here, and that when he passed the test and had finally worked all these years, everything was going to be hunky dory. But just when it looks like his adversity is finally going to end, Jacob's uncle tricks him, and instead of getting Rachel he is given her sister Leah. Without getting into the discussion of how you marry the wrong woman and don't know about it or get into a theological argument about polygamy in the Old Testament, let's stay focused and understand that even in our sin and misunderstanding, God works through our lives. So you mean that Jacob just worked seven years and he didn't even get the girl? Yup, that's right. Of course he confronts Laban about this and Laban makes up some lame excuse about tradition and marrying off the oldest daughter first, blah, blah, blah! He deceived Jacob and now he says that he will give him Rachel in marriage, but he's going to have to work another seven years! And Jacob agrees! At this point a lot of people would have thrown in the towel or decided that they were going to get revenge for this treachery, but not Jacob.   He agrees to the deal, marries Rachel and works another seven years for Laban without bitterness or treachery or deceit.

How was Jacob able to keep a good attitude during these years of hardship and adversity? He kept his eyes on the prize. He was a man of his word, a man of integrity and character and he did what he agreed to at great personal cost. All of us experience adversity. All of us lose focus from time to time. But that is one of the reasons to read this book: to refocus your eyes on Jesus. When we go through adversity and we look at the pain, the pain is magnified. I'm not suggesting that when you're going through something that you don't ask questions or shed your tears. God knows all your questions and He counts all your tears. But at the end of the day, fix your eyes on Jesus so that your pain is minimized and God's power is maximized. I know there may be people reading this book who have felt like Jacob – betrayed, deceived, and tricked. But there is a right way and a wrong way to respond to it. I am not endorsing the door mat policy where you simply let people walk all over you. Jacob confronted Laban about his treachery, but he also controlled his attitude, walked in forgiveness and didn't take revenge. He did not understand why this was happening to him, but to get angry or be vengeful would hot have helped the situation. "*Vengeance is mine says the Lord.*"   (Romans 12:19) Our part is to stay focused, forgive and walk out our Christian life.

As Hebrews puts it – *"Fixing our eyes on Jesus, the author and perfecter of faith"* (Hebrews 12:2a). (NASB) and in Hebrews 3:2 *"He (Jesus) was faithful to Him who appointed Him, as Moses also was in all His house."* (NASB) Just as Jacob was faithful in Laban's house, fix your eyes on Jesus and He will help you be faithful in whatever house you are serving.

God help me to keep my eyes on the prize and on Your Son Jesus Christ. Help me to focus on the prize instead of the negative things that have happened to me. Help me to walk in forgiveness, integrity and character in all adversity that may come my way. Help me to control my attitude so that when adversity comes, I will focus on what You want me to focus on and the time will pass like days.

Review & Begin Weekly Activity

Day 2: Accepting God's Plan

One of the hardest things for us to do as Christians is to accept our circumstances when we are going through adversity. Our first reaction is always to rebuke the devil, believe for healing and to pray for rain so to speak. We should do these things and claim the scriptures and promises of God over our lives. We should confess healing and claim that no harm will befall us and no disease will come near our tent (Psalm 91:10). We need to know that we are more than conquerors (Romans 8:38) and that greater is He who is in us than he who is in the world (1 John 4:4). But when the answer doesn't come and the healing tarries and the rain doesn't fall, what then?

We have to know that God is for us and not against us. (Romans 8:31) We have to know that it is the enemy who comes to steal, kill and destroy. We have to know that God wants to give us an abundant and full life (John 10:10). We have to know that God has plans to prosper us and not to harm us (Jeremiah 29:11) and we have to know that all things work together for good for them that love God (Romans 8:28). At the end of the day when your strength is gone, at the end of the week when your hope is lost and at the end of the year when you don't think you can do it anymore, that is when we must fall into the hands of the living and loving God and confess to Him that we trust Him and believe in Him. We must tell Him we may not understand and we may not enjoy our circumstances, but we trust Him. We know His plans are good for us and we believe in Him.

One of the best examples of this is contained in the story of Job. Let me preface our discussion about Job by asserting that one of the reasons that Job is a good example for us is because we don't necessarily know God's reasons for allowing Satan to attack Job. We can guess and surmise that God wanted to show Satan that man was capable of trusting in Him in the worst of circumstances, or that God wanted to give us an example that was worse than anything any of us will ever experience. That way there will always be something to relate to no matter what our pain. Maybe God wanted to show us that even the best of the best people endure hard times and that it doesn't mean God is punishing us or that He's not pleased with us. Maybe God wanted to give us an example to show us how not to sin when we go through adversity. Or maybe God just wanted to bless Job more than he already was (in the end God blessed him double) and the only way Job was going to appreciate it was if he had perspective about what he already had. Often it is in our nature to ask the question why. But sometimes we have to just trust that His ways are higher than our ways and His thoughts are higher than our thoughts (Isaiah 55:9).

Job was a holy man not like me. He was the real deal Holyfield. He was rich too, like a modern day billionaire tycoon only righteous in all his business dealings without lies or deceit and he never even looked at another woman with lust. All this makes it even harder to understand his pain when he is informed in one day that all of his children are dead and all of his money is gone. For a much more dramatic effect you have to read Job 1 and 2. Then after this, Satan attacks again and Job is struck with a horrible illness with sores all over his body, and the Bible says that in all his adversity he did not sin for he did not blame God.

Job was in tremendous pain and suffering after losing all his possessions and his family, yet Job 1:20ff says, "*Then Job arose and tore his robe and shaved his head, and he fell to the ground and worshipped. He said, 'naked I came from my mother's womb, and naked I shall return there. The Lord gave and the Lord has taken away. Blessed be the name of the Lord.'* In all this Job did not sin nor charge God with wrong."* (NKJV) Did you hear that? He fell to the ground and worshipped. Somehow Job knew that all things work together for good and he could accept his circumstances even though they were painful beyond bearing. He worshipped. He understood the sovereignty of God before sovereignty was a word. He didn't understand why but he knew that ultimately God was in control and that he could trust Him. Even when his wife's faith falters, Job remains faithful. After Job became sick, his wife said to him, "'Do you still hold fast your integrity? Curse God and die.' But he said to her, 'you speak as one of the foolish women speaks. Shall we indeed accept good from God and not accept adversity?' In all this Job did not sin with his lips."* (Job 2:9-10) (NKJV) Sometimes that is the hardest part of accepting God's plan – not knowing why. But that is part of the beauty of the story of Job. We never truly find out why God would allow this to happen, but there are two additional responses during Job's crisis that I think are vital for us to look at and emulate in our adversities.

The first comes in Job 19:23ff. "*Oh that my words were recorded, that they were written on a scroll, that they were inscribed with an iron tool on lead, or engraved in rock forever! I know that my Redeemer lives, and that in the end he will stand upon the earth. And after my skin has been destroyed, yet in my flesh I will see God; I myself will see him with my own eyes – I, and not another. How my heart yearns within me.*" (NIV) Wow! If Job only knew his words were being inscribed with an iron tool and engraved in rock forever. Whatever our pain, whatever our adversities, we can say with all certainty and with all security that I know my Redeemer lives – he lives, he lives, who once was dead, he lives, my ever living friend. Even the worst scenario in this life – death – can not and will not change the fact that our Redeemer Jesus lives and that we will all see Him when we die. And nothing can change the fact that in the end Jesus will stand upon the earth and all dominion, power and authority will be under his feet completely and there will be no more pain, no more suffering and no more tears.

Take comfort in the fact that no matter what you're going through that your Redeemer lives. He's conquered death, sin and the power of the devil. The time is coming when He will stand upon the earth and He will declare ultimate victory forever and ever. As John the revelator said in chapter 20:10ff

"And the devil, who deceived them, was thrown into the lake of burning sulfur, where the beast and the false prophet had been thrown. They will be tormented day and night forever and ever...then I saw a new heaven and a new earth, for the first heaven and the first earth passed away, and there was no longer a sea. I saw the Holy City, the New Jerusalem, coming down out of heaven from God, prepared as a bride beautifully dressed for her husband. And I heard a loud voice from the throne saying, 'Now the dwelling of God is with men, and he will live with them. They will be his people, and God himself will be with them and be their God. He will wipe every tear from their eyes. There will be no more death or mourning or crying or pain, for the old order of things has passed away.' He who was seated on the throne said, 'I am making everything new!' Then he said, 'Write this down for these words are trustworthy and true.' He said to me: 'It is done. I am the Alpha and the Omega, the Beginning and the End. To him who is thirsty I will give drink without cost from the

spring of the water of life. He who overcomes will inherit all this, and I will be his God and he will be my son.' " (NIV)

The other response Job makes that we need to look at is that he comes to a place where he recognizes his frailty in life and he declares that the Lord gives and the Lord takes away, blessed be the name of the Lord. Now we know from having a bird's eye view from the story that it wasn't the Lord that took away – yes the Lord allowed Satan to take away from Job, but it was not God that took all that Job had away. Job didn't know what was going on, but still his response was "Blessed be the name of the Lord." We learn through this extraordinary response that no matter what we may be going through or what we have been through we can say like Job – "Blessed be the name of the Lord." Worship God.

What else is there to say? There are a million questions to ask and ponder if we read the rest of the book of Job. But when it's all said and done let us be like Job and fall down on the ground and worship. In Bible College one of my professors was talking about Saul on the road to Damascus, and he commented that Saul didn't ask why when he was struck with blindness by a great light. He asked two questions. "Who are you Lord" and, "What do you want me to do next?" Let us accept God's good plans for us and trust that all things work together for good.

Lord, help me to accept Your good plans for me and trust that all things work together for my good because I love You. Lord, when things don't go my way, help me not to question why but to focus on who You are and what You want me to do next. In Jesus Name. Amen

Day 3: Faithful With A Few Things

Matthew 25:23 says "*His master replied, 'Well done, good and faithful servant! You have been faithful with a few things; I will put you in charge of many things. Come and share your master's happiness!*" (NIV) Often in our lives we are challenged with being faithful with the little things and we fail to see the connection between being faithful with what God has given us and where God has placed us, and the eventual circumstances that will become our lives. But in the parable of the talents we see clearly that our stewardship with what we have will determine in some way the condition of our future.

In this parable there is a direct connection between what we do with what God gives us, and what will be given to us in the future. There is nothing mystical or magical about knowing our future. It is often a result of the principal of sowing and reaping. What we sow, we will reap. If we sow faithfulness in our stewardship, we will reap abundance. The parable of the talents, located in Matthew 25, says that a master distributed talents to his servants and entrusted his property to them. "*To one he gave five talents of money, to another two talents, and to another one talent, each according to his ability.*" We see then our return on God's investment into our lives is not based on comparing our talents with someone else, it is based on how faithful we are with what we have been given.

The temptation is to compare ourselves to others and to relate that to the rewards we will be given. If we have more gifts and abilities then the temptation is to become prideful and to think that God doesn't expect me to do anything more because we are already "ahead" of others. The other temptation if we have fewer talents than others is to think that we can't make any difference anyway, so why bother trying. The reality is that it doesn't matter how many talents we have, it matters how faithful we are with what we do have.

One of the greatest examples of this in the Bible is the story of Joseph. For those of you that may not be familiar with Joseph's story, we find a man that was faithful in any and all circumstances. Because of this, the Lord continued to promote and reward Joseph all the days of his life. One of the greatest lessons we can extract from Joseph's life is he was always faithful to God, whether he had a lot or a little, and whether he was successful or unsuccessful. Recently I went with my daughter to her children's church program and the children's pastor was talking about the story of Joseph in a message called "There are no accidents." In this message he told the story of Joseph in a very succinct and successful way by using cards that said good or bad. He had children hold the cards and then gave one line statements from Joseph's life that demonstrated how it was a good day or a bad day.

Good – Joseph got a coat

Bad – His brothers hated him

Good – Joseph had a dream

Bad – His brothers tried to kill him

Good – Merchants bought Joseph and took him to Egypt

Bad – Joseph was sold as a slave to Potiphar

Good – The Lord prospered Joseph in everything he did and he was
        in charge of all Potiphar's household

Bad – Potiphar's wife lied about Joseph and he was thrown
        in prison

Good – The Lord was with Joseph and granted him favor so that he
        was put in charge of the whole prison

Bad – Joseph had to stay in prison longer

Good – Joseph interpreted the dreams of the Cupbearer
        and the Baker

Bad – The Cupbearer forgot about Joseph

Good – Joseph interpreted Pharaoh's dream and he was put in
        charge over all of Egypt

Joseph was faithful in all that he did whether he was in the prison or
the palace. Joseph knew his circumstances were not favorable and he
knew that he didn't necessarily do anything to deserve his bad
circumstances, but he remained faithful anyway. Joseph said, *"For I
was forcibly carried off from the land of the Hebrews, and even here I
have done nothing to deserve being put in a dungeon"* (Genesis
40:15). (NIV) Yet that didn't stop him from trusting and serving God
in all that he did. He was faithful in the little things, and he was
faithful when he was over all of Egypt. Nothing deterred Joseph from
being faithful and serving God with all that he had. Good days, bad
days and everything in between – Joseph's external circumstances

didn' t change his internal motivations to serve God and be faithful wherever he was and in whatever he had to do.

We can learn from Joseph' s story that no matter where we are in life or whatever we' re doing, we can be faithful. God doesn' t judge our actions based on anyone else, He simply looks at what we' ve done with what we have. Recently my pastor told a story about Billy Graham and an interview he had with Barbara Walters. The question was asked of him what he wanted to hear God say when he went to heaven. Billy Graham said he wanted to hear God say, "well done good and faithful servant." Barbara Walters was almost dumbfounded because she said surely if anyone will hear well done good and faithful servant it will be you. You' ve preached to more people and had more people accept Jesus than anyone else in history. Graham responded by saying that each person is given assignments from God and his reward will be based on whether he' s been faithful in those assignments, not on what he' s done in comparison to other people.

God' s expectations for you may not be to preach to the nations, but wherever you find yourself and whatever you do, God' s expectations for you are that you are faithful with whatever He' s given you, whether it is large or small. Joseph was unfairly treated, imprisoned, forgotten, and falsely accused but he never used any of those real events in his life as excuses to become unfaithful. Whatever he faced and wherever he was, he was faithful in it all. In what area of your life have you been unfairly treated, forgotten or falsely accused? Have you experienced adverse circumstances? If so, then you need to react like Joseph and still be faithful every single day in every single way. Or maybe you' re having a good day and you' ve been blessed beyond measure. If so, then you need to act like Joseph and be faithful every single day in every single way.

The encouraging thing is that it doesn't matter whether you have been given five talents, two talents or one talent. Your requirement is not to gain as many talents as you can so you can be like so and so. Your requirement is to be faithful with whatever you've been given. Everyone has a calling. Everyone has a vocation and everyone has an assignment to reach hurting people with the love of God and teach people to be more like Christ in whatever sphere of influence that God has given you. There is tremendous freedom in this concept when we realize that we don't have to perform up to the expectations of others or put unnecessary limitations on what we can accomplish. When you stand before God he does not ask you how you did compared to anyone else. He simply asks if you've been faithful with what He's given you and with what He's asked you to do. And when you are faithful with whatever God asks you to do and you stand before the King, you will hear Him say – "Well done, good and faithful servant! You have been faithful with a few things; I will put you in charge of many things. Come and share your master's happiness!"

Dear God, Please help me to be faithful in the things You have given me to do in this season of my life, and even just for today. Help me to be the very best that I can be today no matter what the circumstances are around me - good or bad. Lord, help me to hear Your joy and to share in Your happiness.

Day 4: Praises In The Storm

Having grown up in Michigan, I really appreciate the four seasons even though the joke is that there are only two seasons – winter and construction. But living in the south for the last 5 years, the joke is that there are only two seasons as well – hurricane season and after hurricane season. Storms in general are common, especially in the summer time. But given that we live 6 months out of the year classified as hurricane season – warnings, evacuations and storms become a part of life. We don't really have to discuss the possibility of storms or what causes them, it's a fact they will come. The same is true with the storms of life. Jesus said they would come. It's a fact of life. At the same time that doesn't mean we become storm chasers. There are definitely some self made storms that can be avoided, but the purpose of today's attention is to learn how to respond to the storms in your life. Jesus did say they would come, but He also said "...take heart! I have overcome the world" (John 16:33c).

When Paul and Silas were in Philippi, they were simply going about their business preaching the Gospel. They weren't really planning on walking into a storm. What happened is that Paul cast a spirit out of a girl who predicted the future, and the guys who owned the fortune telling business got really mad and had Paul and Silas thrown in prison. Paul really didn't have a chance to weigh out his options and think to himself, "Well if I cast this spirit out, there's going to be a really big storm so maybe I shouldn't do it." The storm just happened. He didn't know it was coming, but it was a really painful one. The Bible says they were severely beaten, probably similar to how Jesus was flogged, and then they were thrown in the deepest darkest part of the prison with chains all over them.

I doubt you can relate with Paul and Silas who were thrown in jail after being stripped naked and severely beaten, but I'm sure that you can relate with being in a storm. All of us can relate with having trouble, whether it is financial, physical or emotional. We all have experienced trouble. I know you probably have not experienced this exact kind of storm, but you may have experienced agonizing pain. No one's storms are exactly the same, but the pain is similar causing hurts and wounds in similar ways. You may have lost a loved one, experienced gut wrenching excruciating pain, or suffered abuse and neglect that you still have refused to disclose to anyone because of the enormity of your pain. The storms of life come and go, sometimes without warning or cause. But the most important factor with regard to our storms is not how severe the pain is, but the response that we take.

Paul and Silas obviously knew something about experiencing storms. Let's take a look at how they responded in this situation. In Acts 16 verse 25 it says *"About midnight Paul and Silas were praying and singing hymns to God, and the other prisoners were listening to them."* (NIV) What? They were praying and singing praises to God? You mean to tell me they were severely beaten, bleeding profusely, sitting in a deep, dark, cold and moldy dungeon with who knows what kind of animals crawling around and they decide to sing praises to God? That's what it says. I don't know about you, but I know that it isn't just a story. It's absolute truth and that's what the Bible says. Ok, so Paul and Silas were apostles and leaders in the church, but that doesn't give them any more ability to love God or follow Him than you or I have. If you want Bible results than you need to make Bible choices. You have got to make a choice that no matter how much pain, no matter how bad or how big your storm, you are going to praise God. He knows what you're going through. He sees your tears and He feels your pain, but He didn't cause it. He wants to heal it.

I know it's tough and that it might feel funny to praise God in the midst of your storm, but whoever said that you should always listen to your feelings? Always listen to your conscience yes, but your feelings may be contrary to what you need to do. Do you think that Paul and Silas felt like singing praises to God? Psalm 34 says, "*I will bless the Lord at all times.*" (NASB) It says I will. You have got to step out and make a choice that no matter how you feel or no matter what your circumstances, you are going to give praise to God. When things aren't going your way or when you are going through extreme pain and suffering, you have got to make a choice that you will bless the Lord at all times.

So what happened with Paul and Silas when they made a choice to praise God in the midst of their pain? Verse 26 tells us "S*uddenly there was such a violent earthquake that the foundations of the prison were shaken. At once all the prison doors flew open, and everybody's chains came loose.*" (NIV) It was not a coincidence that while they were singing praises to God an earthquake came that delivered them. So often in our lives we try to minimize, alleviate or escape the pain in our lives. That just brings more focus and power to the pain. The best response is to focus on the one who can take the pain away, and when we do that I believe God will bring a great deliverance in your life just like He did for Paul and Silas. Notice that when Paul and Silas made a decision to praise God, not only were their chains loosed, but the Bible says everybody's chains came loose. When we praise God in the midst of our storms then those around us will also experience deliverance in their lives because of the miraculous power of God. And there is another benefit as well. Not only will we and others around us experience deliverance, but there will be treasures that are taken from the kingdom of darkness that would not have been accessible without praising God in the midst of the storms in our life. When Paul and Silas praised God and everyone's chains were loosed, the jailer was extremely discouraged, and Paul and Silas were able to minister to him and he and his whole family were saved. There probably would have been no other way that God would have been able to reach this man and his family. They needed to see the miraculous power of God. If Paul and Silas would have gone up to him on the street without any prior contact, he probably would have dismissed them. But when he saw the power of God manifested in their lives, he and his family were plundered from the kingdom of darkness and delivered into the kingdom of God.

Paul and Silas' focus was not on escaping or they would have run when the doors were open. It even says that they returned to the prison after they went to the jailer's home. So we can see that our motives and our focus should not always be on our release. God will deliver you when your attention and your focus are on Him and His purposes. When our attention and our focus is on God and seeking His face, that is precisely when He will release His hand to deliver you.

Some tragedies are so great and painful that any response we take seems insignificant, like with the earthquake in Haiti. When there is such utter desolation and destruction, any response we give seems flippant and naïve. There are some pains so great and some hurts so deep that our only response is to weep with those who weep and fall back into the arms of a loving God who knows more than we do and is sovereignly in control.   Thankfully, we don't live under the Old Testament covenant anymore and God is not up in heaven creating plans to destroy humanity. He is figuring out how to draw all men unto Himself. But until that time comes completely, we still live in a fallen world where tragedy transpires and the devil comes to steal, kill and destroy.   And when we sit in the darkness of the dungeon or the ashes of tragedy we can only say "*God is our refuge and strength, a very present help in trouble. Therefore we will not fear, though the earth give way and the mountains fall into the heart of the sea, though its waters roar and foam and the mountains quake with their surging.... 'Be still, and know that I am God; I will be exalted among the nations, I will be exalted in the earth' "* (Psalm 46:1-3,10). (NKJV)

Lord, please deliver me from my pain and suffering. But more than that, Lord, I ask that You give me a heart that praises You in every season of life. When storms come in my life help me to remember this story and focus my attention on You and Your goodness. Help me to believe You for deliverance for me and those around me.

Day 5: Suffering For The Name

Please don't think by reading this title that I am somehow endorsing the desire to experience suffering. Certainly God has paid the price through His son Jesus who suffered enough for all of us. Through His death and resurrection He took the sin, the death, the sickness and the suffering that we all deserved. We can now walk in victory over these things because of the blood of Jesus.

I am not endorsing purposeful suffering, self-flagellation or permanent vows of isolation or poverty that bring pain and suffering upon ones self. Yet still we live in a fallen world and there is sin, death, sickness and suffering that will not be fully relinquished from the earth until Jesus returns again. But this is not the type of suffering that I am suggesting we experience – the kind that says I'm just suffering for Jesus. Jesus doesn't want you to suffer. He wants you to be healed. At the same time there is a type of suffering that we can be thankful for. It's hard to imagine being thankful for suffering, but there is biblical precedence for it.

In Acts chapter 5 the apostles had been arrested for preaching that Jesus had risen from the dead and that He was the Savior. Verse 19 and 20 say, *"But during the night an angel of the Lord opened the gates of the prison, and taking them out he said, 'Go, stand and speak to the people in the temple the whole message of this Life."* (NASB) So even though they had just been arrested for preaching the Gospel, they went right back to the temple and began preaching publicly again. The apostles were arrested again, questioned and the council of the high priest was considering putting them to death. But instead they were warned, beaten and then released. Verse 41&42

says that after they left from just being beaten and probably whipped 39 times, "...*they went on their way from the presence of the Council, rejoicing that they had been considered worthy to suffer shame for His name. And every day, in the temple and from house to house, they kept right on teaching and preaching Jesus as the Christ.*" (NASB) There it is. The apostles rejoiced in their suffering. They were joyful and thankful about suffering for the name of Jesus. Not that they went looking for it, but when it happened they considered it a joy and an honor to suffer for their master Jesus.

Where did the apostles find their strength to continue to preach the gospel in the face of such opposition? Why didn't they pack up, go home and say, "Ok we need to do this another way or in another place?" We see plenty of times in scripture where the disciples wavered in their faith and rather than being thankful in adversity they gave in to their fear. In Mark 14:50, scripture tells us Jesus' disciples forsook Him and fled in fear. In Matthew 26, Peter, one of Jesus' closest friends, denied Him three times. In John 19 we see the disciples hiding in the upper room after Jesus' crucifixion for fear of the Jews. What was so different now that they were able to stand in the face of adversity and proclaim their praise to God? I think we can find our answer in John 14:26-27. "*But the Counselor, the Holy Spirit, whom the Father will send in my name, will teach you all things and will remind you of everything I have said to you. Peace I leave with you; my peace I give you. I do not give to you as the world gives. Do not let your hearts be troubled and do not be afraid.*" (NIV) After Jesus ascended into Heaven, in Acts 2 we see the coming of the Holy Spirit. Jesus told them the Holy Spirit would come to be their helper, to bring peace and to take away their fear. Of course! Their complete disposition had changed because of the power of the Holy Spirit. But still, why risk such suffering? When they were asked this question by the Jewish authorities, "Peter and the apostles answered, 'we must obey God rather than men' " (Acts 5:29).

They had to obey God. They could do no other. So how does this possibly apply to us since most of you reading this can talk about Jesus freely without negative consequence (and for that we ought to be thankful)? What about when it's illegal to pass out Bibles or illegal to share your faith with someone else in another country? Don't think that these are isolated instances not applicable to our own lives. Although most of us don't face the reality of imprisonment or torture, there is a reality of suffering for the name of Jesus that we are to rejoice in when it happens. For me it looks like working at a place where my boss asks me not to pray for people. For you it might look like not praying in the name of Jesus at an event or at school. It might look like having an accountant that encourages you to be dishonest about your taxes, or having a financial planner that discourages you from tithing. Or maybe it's someone asking you to teach something in opposition to the Bible. As a young person, maybe it looks like being made fun of for not drinking or for being a virgin, or maybe being disgraced by a teacher or another student because you stood up for creationism. "*Blessed are those who have been persecuted for the sake of righteousness, for theirs is the kingdom of Heaven*" (Matthew 5:10). (NASB)

There is a possibility you may be discouraged because you know you haven't been thankful in everything at all times. Ok – let's be realistic. It's challenging to be thankful in everything at all times. We can't do it on our own. But that's where the Holy Spirit becomes our Helper. The Holy Spirit is given to us as Christians. The Holy Spirit gives us the power to be thankful, to see the benefit of being thankful, to be obedient to God and to feel God's pleasure. In

Ephesians 5 verse 20 it says "always giving thanks to God the Father for everything in the name of our Lord Jesus Christ." You may be wondering if you' re taking all of this being thankful stuff seriously, how you can do it. There is a Biblical principal you need to remember. God will never ask you to do something that is impossible for you to do. He will always enable you to accomplish what He asks of you. "How," you may wonder? In the verse before which God instructs us to always give thanks, he tells us 'don' t get drunk on wine, which leads to debauchery. Instead, be filled with the Holy Spirit.' Be filled with the Holy Spirit who gives you the strength to be what you can not be, to say what you can not say, and to obey when you can not obey on your own.

Obviously, being obedient to God does not mean that we as Christians should always be confrontational and argumentative, for love must rule. There is a time to speak and a time to listen. But whenever you are confronted with the choice of obeying God or man, I pray that you will find the strength to obey God, and when you suffer for the name of Jesus, you will find the joy to give thanks for your suffering. *"Rejoice and be glad for your reward in heaven is great; for in the same way they persecuted the prophets who were before you"* (Matthew 5:12).(NASB)

Lord please fill me with Your Holy Spirit. Give me the strength to obey You rather than men. When my obedience leads to suffering help me to be thankful and rejoice for suffering for the name of Your Son, and help me to feel Your pleasure in my obedience.

Day 6: Take Up Your Cross

I guess you could say that I've saved the best for last because really there can be no better example for us on how to handle anything than our Savior Jesus. But my challenge is to make the story of this day fresh and new as I tell the "old, old story." How many times have you heard that Jesus died on the cross for you? How many times have you heard that Jesus rose from the dead? It's still miraculous. It's still powerful. It's still the greatest story ever told and my prayer is that as you see Jesus' response to adversity today that it will give you a new appreciation of His sacrifice and a renewed vigor to take up your cross in your own life.

What's amazing to me is that Jesus knew it all, but He did it anyway with a submitted and willing heart. What I mean by that is Jesus knew His life would end in suffering and death, and he volunteered to leave heaven and come to earth anyway. He knew Judas would betray Him, yet He chose him as one of His disciples. He knew His disciples would desert Him, yet He poured His life into them. He knew Peter would deny Him, but He called him the rock. He knew that everyone would turn on Him when they yelled crucify Him, yet He healed and taught like a man who trusted everyone. And He knew His time was near, but still He went to celebrate the Passover. Jesus knew that Judas had already agreed to betray Him, but still He washed his feet and called him friend.

Even though the disciples didn't get it, Jesus kept telling them over and over again that He must suffer and die. (Matt. 16:21-23; Mark 8:31-33; Luke 9:21-22). But still there was a joy, a contentment and a thankfulness that Jesus demonstrated even though He knew suffering and death loomed around the corner. Luke

22:15 says *"I have eagerly desired to eat this Passover with you before I suffer."* (NIV) Jesus knew how to give himself fully to the moment at hand and was completely full of love and thankfulness with betrayal, desertion and suffering staring Him in the face. Jesus knew His suffering was imminent yet He lived gratefully anyway. He spent the very night of His arrest serving His disciples, celebrating the Passover and singing and praying with them. *"When they had sung a hymn, they went out to the Mount of Olives"* (Mark 14:26). (NIV) Jesus didn' t only accept His adversity, He embraced it and lived His very last moments with His disciples to the fullest, giving thanks for the Last Supper and worshipping and praising God with His disciples as He sang a hymn.

We know that Jesus went to the Mount of Olives and He prayed fervently, even with the sweat of blood, that this cup of suffering would be taken away from Him. He wouldn' t have been human if He didn' t do that. Jesus didn' t want to suffer, but He was willing to suffer. Jesus wished there was another way. Jesus wanted to continue to live and breathe and spend time with His friends and family, but He was willing to do whatever it took and whatever the Father asked of Him. He was willing to take up His cross. Jesus set aside His desires and His wishes and put them in the Father' s hands and said not my will, but your will be done. Jesus didn' t do what He wanted to, Jesus was willing to do what was asked of Him.

I remember a time after our family had moved to the New Orleans area. We felt very strongly that God had called us down there, but I remember kind of complaining. We had sold and given up everything to go to Bible school in St. Louis, MO, and now just a few years later we were starting all over again. We felt like God was asking us to once again give up everything. I remember complaining about this in my head and just asking the Lord how many times are we going to have to do this and start over again? And His response surprised me when He said – **daily** take up your cross and follow me. It was so clear- yet so foreign. I thought that just because we had given up everything to follow God, it was a one time event and that was it. But how wrong I was.

The other time that was a real season of suffering in my life was when I was working at a fast food restaurant. I remember the Lord telling me that I wasn't going to be there anymore, and I immediately thought that meant I was going on to something bolder and better (which was not the case). I didn't want to go. I enjoyed my job, the people I worked with and I was making very good money. But I remember so clearly meditating one morning, as I was cooking over the grill, on the posture of Jesus. His posture needed to be my posture - not my will but your will Lord. Jesus didn't want to go to the cross, but He was willing to go. I may not understand it or want it, but I am willing to accept God's will above my will. Thank God for the example of His perfect Son Jesus, who committed no sin and did no wrong, but was deserted, betrayed and put to death. Thank you, Jesus for living the perfect life and being the perfect example on how to take up your cross. There is no one like you. There is none like you Lord.

It was incredibly painful to lose my job, and within six months time – I had lost my job, had back surgery for a ruptured disc, my wife had emergency surgery for a tubal pregnancy and we lost our house to foreclosure. But in that time God showed up in miraculous ways and healed my back, paid off all of our debt, gave us a car and set us up in a house with more room, in a better school district and for less money. And God put a seed in my heart for this book because part of the reason that I lost my job was because I wasn't thankful for it. So even when it appears that there may be great hardship at hand, when we take up our cross God always works everything out for our good. The enemy may intend it for evil, but God has good plans for you. He showed our family that no matter what we go through, He will always be there for us and always provide for us. God's loving kindness endures forever, and His faithfulness is from generation to generation.

Look at what happened to Jesus when He took up His cross. Yes, He suffered immeasurably even though He deserved none of it, but He rose from the dead and conquered death, sin and the devil. And not only is He now in glory with the Father, but He made a way for everyone who believes in Him to live in heaven forever. When we are obedient to take up whatever cross God asks us to take up, there is always great blessing, great reward and great provision attached to that cross enabling us to walk through what God is asking us to walk through. Not that we look for suffering or think God would ask us to take up a cross of sin to show His grace, may it never be. But we look for opportunities of obedience to step forward into whatever God is calling us to, no matter what anybody else thinks or no matter who is on your side. If God is for you, who can be against you?

John 18:4 from the New Living Translation says, "*Jesus fully realized all that was going to happen to him, so he stepped forward to meet them.*" He wanted it to go another way and even prayed that it would go another way, and then Judas showed up. Jesus didn't run or disappear through the crowd as He had done at other times, and He didn't call thousands of angels which were at His disposal. Jesus didn't complain, didn't ask why and didn't come up with any excuses – Jesus fully realized what was going to happen and He **stepped forward**!

God may have asked you to do something difficult in your life or He may be asking you right now as you're reading this, "Will you go for me?" There are a lot of responses that you could come up with and there are a lot of reactions that you could have, but I encourage you to follow the example of Jesus and step forward into the plans and purposes that God has for you. Take up your cross and follow Him. Not that you desire suffering, but that you are willing and obedient to take the path that God has asked you to take even, if it is more difficult or even if it's the road less traveled by.

Lord please give me the strength to take up my cross in life. Help me to understand that Your yoke is easy and Your burden is light, and any path You ask me to take, that may be difficult, will be filled with Your protection, Your provision and Your blessing. Show me right now what cross I need to take up in my life, and show me how to step forward.

Complete & Reflect On Weekly Activity

WEEK 4

GIVING THANKS IN

REAPING

Day 1: Introduction &
Count Your Returns (Blessings)

It's very common to hear people talk about karma in today's world or they may say what goes around comes around. The belief is that whatever things you do, they will be done to you. This belief is true because it is a Biblical principle. The reason so many people talk about it and believe it is because they see it in their lives and in the lives of others. It is called the law of sowing and reaping. *"For whatever a man sows, that he will also reap"* (Galatians 6:7b). (NKJV) You can call it whatever you want, but the truth is that the idea came from God and it's His principle. You reap what you sow.

At the same time God is a good and gracious God and we often receive more than we can ask or imagine because of His grace and favor in our lives. Both principles are true. There is 1) the law of sowing and reaping and 2) God blesses us and gives us grace just because we are His children. Whatever the reason for you reaping a blessing there is no better time to thank the Lord. One of the best examples of someone taking time to thank the Lord when they reaped a great blessing comes from the story of the ten lepers.

Luke 17:12 *"Then as He [Jesus] entered a certain village, there met Him ten men who were lepers, who stood afar off. And they lifted up their voices and said, 'Jesus, Master, have mercy on us!' So when He saw them, He said to them, 'Go, show yourselves to the priests.' And so it was that as they went, they were cleansed."* (NKJV) Ten lepers cried out to Jesus for mercy and He told them to go show themselves to the priest. And **on their way** they were healed. Lepers were despised and degraded and were not allowed in main stream society because of their contagious skin disease. These lepers were not only crying out to be healed but asking for mercy so that they could again experience fellowship, love and human interaction with family and friends. The interesting thing about their healing is that it wasn't an immediate, awe inspiring miracle. There weren't lights from heaven or visions of angels or even the overpowering presence of God. At least not that we know of. The Bible says that as they went they were cleansed. At some point along the way they must have noticed that they were healed because one of them came back to thank Jesus. Some went to show their friends and family, some went into town to celebrate and some may have gone looking for a job but one went back to thank Jesus. Verses 15-16 *"And one of them, when he saw that he was healed, returned, and with a loud voice glorified God, and fell down on his face at His feet, giving Him thanks. And he was a Samaritan."* (NKJV)

After reading the story again, I started to think about my own life and wondered how many miracles or answered prayers that I've never taken the time to go back and thank Jesus for. How many times have I prayed and God answered my prayer as I went **on my way** and I had forgotten that I even prayed about it? Or how many times has God miraculously answered my prayers in an unassuming and inconspicuous way that I haven't acknowledged? Or how many times has God answered my prayers but I was too busy, focused on something else, or too lazy to go back and thank Him for all He's done?

God is so good. He has so much in mind for you and for your life – more than you can ask or imagine. God doesn't like to do what we ask. He likes to do more than we ask. He is not a genie that grants your wishes. He wants to bless you and bless you indeed, but it could be an intangible gift like the attitude of someone in your family or an encouraging word or good health or blessed children. It is better to just ask God to bless you and let Him decide how He wants to bless you. I've figured out that God doesn't really like to be told how to bless you. He's the daddy. He's creative. He's imaginative. So instead of demanding your way – ask for His way. It's kind of like taking Bill Gates to the dollar store and saying this is what I want! This is it; this is what I really have my heart set on. He tries to interrupt you and say "let's go to the mall and I'll let you pick out whatever you...." But you are so insistent and don't listen to what he's saying. Instead you exclaim, "No, no this is what I want please, please." Trust God that He has good plans for you. Trust Him with your life. He wants you to succeed more than you do. He's cheering for you and He's trying to help you.

For your week 4 activity I would like you to pray about giving a thanksgiving offering to the Lord, something that tells Him - thank you; something that shows Him you recognize that every good and perfect gift comes from Him. Something to show Him you haven't forgotten and He matters most. It's not a bribe and I'm not asking you to give beyond what you are able. And don't even think about laying something at His feet in dishonesty like in Acts 5 with Ananias and Sapphira. Make it a gift from the heart and an offering to the Lord, a sweet smelling aroma. This is not your tithe to your home church, it is an offering over and above your tithe. Be creative. It doesn't have to be money – it could be time – it could be a project – it could be anything. If you're married, talk about it with your spouse and if your spouse doesn't feel comfortable about it, then don't fight about it. Do something else that both of you are comfortable with. The point is to give a thanks offering to the Lord, telling Him how much you appreciate everything He has done for you in your life. Take some time out to thank Him with a gift this week. Write down some ideas and then take some time to pray, decide and follow through with a gift from your heart.

Count Your Returns (Blessings)

Being thankful for your blessings is the easiest time to be thankful, but it is also the easiest time to forget to be thankful. We have something that we practice with our children. If they don't say thank you for what they get then occasionally we will take it away. It might be candy or an ice cream cone or whatever, but if they forget to say thank you and we take it away they know why. It is a hard lesson sometimes, but they don't forget very often after that happens a couple of times. The challenge for them is their eyes get so big and they concentrate so much on the gift that they're getting they forget about the giver. Once it registers they immediately say, "Thank you, thank you, thank you!" Almost like, "How could I forget to say thank you for such a great gift?", but they forget because they were focusing on the gift and not the giver. Unfortunately, the same thing happens to us with God. We can get so caught up in the blessing, enjoying it and thinking about it and how great it is that we can forget to thank the giver who gave us the gift.

I remember when my wife and I were living in St. Louis going to Bible College. We were so incredibly blessed. One of my best friends at the college was from St. Louis and his dad had season tickets to almost all the pro sporting events. Then my wife worked for a major corporation as an assistant for one of the big wigs and she would get tickets all the time as well. We were going to baseball games, hockey games and all kinds of other events any time we wanted while we were making very little money and going to Bible

College. At the time I didn't think much of it because I had grown up going to pro sporting events. But now I realize how unbelievably blessed we were. It was easy to say thank you to my friend and the company Michelle worked for, but I know I wasn't nearly as thankful to God as I should have been. Unfortunately sometimes, you don't know what you have until it's gone. But that is part of why we are studying about being thankful so that we can be thankful right here right now and not repenting that we weren't thankful later.

Part of remembering to be thankful is determining to get rid of the "if only's."   If only I had another car, if only I had a nicer home, if only I had a better cell phone, if only I had a bigger TV, etc., etc. As I read in a little children's book called <u>The Secret of Saying Thanks</u> by Douglas Wood we are not thankful because we are happy, we are happy because we are thankful. Happiness is one of those illusive concepts that the more you try to pursue it the further it seems to slip from your grasp. But if you are thankful right where you are, you will find that happiness will come to you when you aren't chasing it.

My brother is a financial planner and one of his primary objectives is to give his clients a good return on their investments. Although my brother is an excellent financial planner with high level executives with major corporations as clients, and has an excellent portfolio, the returns are not always good especially in a bad economy: but that hasn't changed the goal – good returns. There will be times in our lives when we don't have good returns and the blessings seem to tarry, but that doesn't change God's feelings toward us and it doesn't nullify His promises in our lives. The goal is still to live in His blessing of health and financial provision and peace and joy.

Recently, Michelle and I had been challenged with having one vehicle for our family. We had a minor accident with no injuries, but it cost us $1,000 more than our insurance coverage. At the time Michelle was in between jobs and there was no way we could pay for it. All we could do was pray. God knew what had happened and He was able to help us. We could have turned to our parents or we could have seen about getting a credit card or we could have asked for a loan from a friend. There may be times to do any of those things in an emergency and we have in the past, but this time we felt led by God to totally trust in Him and let Him handle it.

It was not an easy process and for much of the two plus months without the vehicle we were unclear about what to do, but God knew what He was going to do. Some friends of ours knew our situation and offered to lend us their truck that they weren' t using at the time, which was a huge blessing to us. As we waited on the Lord He miraculously provided for our needs. Then without my bringing it up, my dad asked out of nowhere how the new van had been running. Now He hadn' t asked about it in two months but that day on our anniversary he asked. I told him what had happened and he talked with Michelle' s dad and they decided to split the cost to fix it so we could get the van back! What a blessing! God uses people to accomplish His will, but the blessing comes from trusting in God. We need to call on God not on man. Don' t concentrate on the gift or the person that God uses to give the gift, put your trust in the Lord and thank Him. Thank you Lord for the money to fix our van! When your investment is with God and you sow trust in Him, He brings good returns. When the good returns come and when you get exactly what you want, when the blessing of your life comes along, train yourself to concentrate on the giver and not the gift. In Isaiah 38 we see a great example of this. Hezekiah was a godly king, but he became ill and asked Isaiah the prophet to come and pray for him. Isaiah came and told him he should put his house in order because he was going to die. Hezekiah wept before the Lord and cried out to God asking Him to spare His life, reminding God how he had served Him faithfully. The Bible says in 2 Kings 20,

> *"Before Isaiah had gone out of the middle court, the word of the Lord came to him, saying, 'Return and say to Hezekiah the leader of My people, 'Thus says the Lord, the God of your father David, 'I have heard your prayer, I have seen your tears; behold, I will heal you. On the third day you shall go up to the house of the Lord. 'I will add fifteen years to your life, and I will deliver you and this city from the hand of the king of Assyria; and I will defend this city for My own sake and for My servant David's sake.' "* (NASB)

Hezekiah is incredibly grateful for his gift, but he doesn't throw a great banquet in Isaiah's honor. He recognizes that this gift has come from God and he thanks Him with a special poem that he writes for the Lord. This poem is recorded in scripture in Isaiah 38. Take a look at it some time. Hezekiah got exactly what he was praying for and he admirably turned to the Lord and gave Him praise and thanksgiving for this great gift. When your blessing comes, thank the Lord with all your heart and praise Him in His mighty heavens.

The challenge when you receive your blessing is to remain focused. The Israelites faced this challenge after God delivered them from the Egyptians. It was a miraculous deliverance after 400 years of slavery. There were the plagues, the parting of the Red Sea, the destruction of the Egyptian army and then manna and quail - it was amazing and miraculous. God had miraculously delivered them against all odds and in one of the most awe inspiring and captivating acts of God in the Bible, Israel had been set free from Egyptian slavery once and for all.

So what was going to happen now that all of their prayers had been answered and they had exactly what they were hoping for? That's where we pick up in Exodus 19. *"In the third month after the sons of Israel had gone out of the land of Egypt, on that very day they came into the wilderness of Sinai."* (NASB) Just three short months after the parting of the Red Sea, Israel came to Mount Sinai and God gave Moses the 10 commandments. After Moses presented the law to Israel they agreed and affirmed their covenant with God. Then God told Moses to come back up the mountain with Aaron, Nadab, Abihu and seventy of the elders. So they went up the mountain to worship the Lord and the Lord called Moses to come up higher, so he and Joshua went further. (Exodus 24:15-18)

> *"Then Moses went up to the mountain, and the cloud covered the mountain. The glory of the Lord rested on Mount Sinai, and the cloud covered it for six days; and on the seventh day He called to Moses from the midst of the cloud. And to the eyes of the sons of Israel the appearance of the glory of the Lord was like a consuming fire on the mountain top. Moses entered the midst of the cloud as he went up to the mountain; and Moses was on the mountain forty days and forty nights."* (NASB)

Now remember this was only about four or five months after the parting of the Red Sea, one of the most incredible miracles in the entire Bible. So while Moses is on the mountain top what do you think the Israelites were doing? Were they still so unbelievably thankful and in awe that they were just worshipping God and waiting for their leader to return? Well not exactly. Instead of throwing a party to thank God, they were in the midst of having a revelry party and worshipping a golden calf. They had lost their focus and forgot their deliverer.

So whether you have received intangible blessings, financial blessings, healing or you have been delivered from your enemies, focus on the giver and not the gift. Thank God for answering your prayer and for the miracle of life. Realize how incredibly blessed you are, and have been, and give thanks to the giver of all. *"Shout joyfully to the Lord, all the earth. Serve the Lord with gladness; Come before Him with joyful singing. Know that the Lord Himself is God; It is He who has made us, and not we ourselves; We are His people and the sheep of His pasture."* (Psalm 100:1-3). (NASB) Focus on what you have and not on what you don't have. It's a matter of perspective. If you focus on everything that you don't have but want, it will be very difficult to be thankful. But if you can focus on everything that you do have and recall the blessings of God in your life, your thankfulness will shine forth like the dawn of a new day and you can bring a gift that is a pleasing aroma to Him.

Father God, I praise You for all You are and all You do for me. I'm humbled at the blessings You shower me with every day, and I ask for Your forgiveness for the times I may have been enamored with the gift and not the giver. You truly are my Jehovah Jireh, my God who provides. Lord, help me to always be thankful toward You the giver. Amen.

Review & Begin Weekly Activity

Day 2: The Golden Rule

Most of you are probably familiar with the Golden Rule. Do unto others as you would have them do unto you (Luke 6:31). I believe that this is not only a rule it is also a principle that is included in the law of sowing and reaping. If you treat others with kindness, trust and respect, then people will treat you with kindness, trust and respect. If you honor, love and cherish others, then for the most part, you can expect others will honor, love and cherish you. I'm not saying you go up to someone, treat them kindly and the next person will treat you kindly. But there is an overarching principle of sowing and reaping that pertains to all of life. I have seen this in my grandma's life. She was one of the most caring, loving and serving individuals I have ever had the privilege of knowing. Now that she is 98 and incapable of caring for herself, she has a hospice nurse that comes to take care of her, a neighbor that helps all the time, a doctor that comes to visit her on a regular basis and one of her sons and daughters-in-law live with her to care for her, not to mention my mom and all of her family that visits.

If you care for others then others will care for you. It's part of the blessing that is attached to obedience. It's not that there is something "magical" about being nice to others – it's about being obedient. If we listen and follow God's word for our lives – whatever the command - then there will be a blessing attached to it. If God tells us to do unto others as we would have them do unto us, we need to obey. If God tells us to honor our father and mother, we need to obey. If God tells us do not lie, we need to obey. There is blessing attached to obedience to the word of God.

That's why it is so much more important to be obedient than to be rich, or successful, or popular or pretty. Not that there is anything wrong with those things, but when they come at the expense of not being obedient, then we understand Jesus' question – "*What does it profit a man to gain the whole world and to forfeit his soul?*" (Mark 8:36) The most important quality you can implement into your life, into your children's lives and into your grandchildren's lives is obedience to God. Then you will know the blessing of the Lord. "*Knowing that whatever good anyone does, he will receive the same from the Lord*" (Eph 6:8). "*He who trusts in the Lord will be prospered*" (Prov.28:25). "*No good thing will He withhold from those who walk uprightly*" (Psalm 84:11). "*Fear the Lord you His saints. There is no want to those who fear Him*" (Psalm 34:9). "*And all these blessings shall come upon you and overtake you, because you obey the voice of the Lord your God*" (Deut. 28:2).

Let me be clear about what we are talking about here. We are not talking about being saved. Being saved has nothing to do with what you do or your obedience to the Word. Being saved is Jesus plus nothing. Trusting and believing in Jesus is the only way to be saved and the only way to get to heaven. There is no amount of obedience, no amount of good works or any amount of good intentions that will save you. It is by believing in Jesus and His death and resurrection that you are saved, and knowing that He died for you and your sins. If you don't know beyond a shadow of a doubt that you are going to heaven, then no amount of good works can change that.

This is not to say that everything we do doesn't matter. It just doesn't matter with regard to us being saved. There are eternal rewards to be earned and there are earthly blessings that will follow obedient actions. It's kind of like in the game of golf. When you pay your greens fee they give you a scorecard. Whether you score 140 or 60 you are still in the game and you won't be kicked off the course. However, there are a lot of rules in golf and depending how well you know the rules and follow them will largely determine your score. If you're a golfer then you know that officially there are no mulligan's (redo's) and there is a stroke and distance penalty for when you hit your ball outside the white stakes. There is a penalty for touching the sand with your club before you strike the ball. There is a penalty for putting the ball in the hole with the flag still in the cup. There is a penalty for moving your ball and improving your lie. You get the point. There are a lot of rules to follow.

Now imagine that every time you play there is someone watching your every move. No matter how discretely you cheat, that person sees every rule you break and sees what you are doing. When you finish and turn in your scorecard he automatically adds those penalties to your score. You may even break rules that you didn't know existed. But that is what the scorekeeper is for. He is completely just and completely fair and he's not going to add any points to your scorecard unless you break the rules. He won't show favoritism and he won't cheat you. When we get to heaven it may be something like that. According to Jesus, the Judge, there will be a separation of the sheep and the goats (Matt. 25:31-36) and the most important factor will be if you are "in the game" or not. But there will also be a reckoning of our actions once we are in the game that will determine our eternal rewards and that influence our blessing in this life.

When you turn in your scorecard at the end of the game and say, "Here, I got an 80" a lot of us may be surprised when the Judge turns on his video player and says, "Well you committed a penalty here, and you had an extra stroke there, so you actually got a 102, but the greens fee has been paid so don't worry about your scorecard you can use mine." I imagine it might be similar to that when we end our game of life and are confronted with all the mistakes we have made and all of the good things we could have done but failed to do. In the grace and mercy of God, He will say, "Don't worry about it. You believe in Jesus and He already paid the fees for you. Well done good and faithful servant, enter into your master's happiness."

At the same time we need to realize that there is still a recording taking place and there will be rewards given based on how well we score. *"For we must all appear before the judgment seat of Christ, that each one may receive what is due him for the things done while in the body, whether good or bad"* (2Cor. 5:10). (NIV) With regard to our eternal rewards at the end of the game of life, it doesn't matter how much we know the Word – it matters how much of the Word that we implement in our lives. The same goes for golf. If you became an expert about the rules of golf and you could quote every PGA rule verbatim but when you played golf you didn't follow the rules your score would be poor. You would have to not only know the rules but also follow them in order for you to have a better score.

Deuteronomy 30:11ff it says *"Now what I am commanding you today is not too difficult for you or beyond your reach....See, I set before you today life and prosperity, or death and destruction. For I command you today to love the Lord your God, to walk in his ways, and to keep his commands, decrees and laws; then you will live and increase, and the Lord your God will bless you in the land you are entering to possess."* (NIV)   When you sow obedience you reap blessing but when you sow disobedience you reap destruction. The most important factor is our motive for being obedient and our faith demonstrated through love, but no matter how pure our motives are if we are not obedient, we will reap the consequences of our choices. But if you are obedient Jesus said that you would be blessed.   *"He replied, 'Blessed rather are those who hear the word of God and obey it' "* (Luke 11:28). Jesus didn't say you'd be blessed if you forwarded ten emails or if you prayed a sacred prayer although I'm all for emails about God and prayers without ceasing, but Jesus said you would be blessed if you hear the word of God and obey it. He didn't say that you'd be blessed if you carried a "holy" cross or as they tried to say about His mom that you'd be blessed if you gave birth to a preacher. From Jesus own mouth He said "you'd be blessed if you heard the word of God and obeyed it."

God didn't give us His commandments because He is a giant killjoy. He gave us His commandments to protect us from the consequences of sin and to help us live in blessing and peace. God didn't say, "Do not commit adultery" to stop you from being happy. He commanded that because he knows how difficult it is to be a single parent and He knows the heartache and pain attached to divorce. God didn't say, "Do not lie" to stop you from having fun. He said it so that your conscience could be clear so you would be free from anxiety, and so that you wouldn't have broken relationships and hurt feelings. God didn't say, "Honor your father and mother" so you'd have to live a restricted life and miss out on all the excitement. He said it so that it would be well with you and so that you would live long on the earth. God wants the very best for you and everything He commands you to do in His word is for your benefit and for your blessing. But you have to trust Him and you have to believe He wants what's best for you. Otherwise you'll go your own way and when you have a decision to make between what feels right or what God's word says, you'll be tempted to choose death and destruction for the pleasure of the moment. But if you trust Him and believe that He wants the very best for you, then you can say no to the immediate carrot dangling in your face and choose life and prosperity that God will bring you when you do it His way. The good news is that there is always forgiveness and restoration for those of us who have made bad choices. So this day determine in your heart that you are going to choose life. Determine that you are going to trust God and His word and that you are going to be a doer of the word of God and not just a hearer only. And for all of the bad choices that you've made, be released in the name of Jesus – the name that is above every name. May every curse be broken, every rough place made smooth and every condemnation end. May the power of the blood of Jesus heal every heartache, forgive every mistake and bind every wound.

The consequences of our choices played out in our family recently with our girls. We were getting ready for church one Sunday morning and we were going to take two vehicles because I had to go to work afterward. Because I'm not around as much as mom it's sort of special to ride with dad so all three girls asked to ride with me. Usually, I do it based on whoever asks first and make them take turns, but on this particular occasion I used this scenario to make the point that good behavior is rewarded. One of my girls hadn't listened that morning and one of them had not completed her Sunday School assignment which we had talked about on several occasions. So I told them I was going to let the other sister ride who had listened and finished her assignment. I was blessing the good behavior. I was not mad or unloving toward my other two daughters. They are my children and I love them. But for this particular moment I chose to esteem my daughter who had been obedient.

We see from Scripture that there is a blessing attached to obedience (Matthew 7:24-25). And we all know from our own experiences that there are consequences to our poor decisions. There is a law of sowing and reaping. And it is also true that sometimes bad things happen to holy men and women of God and good things happen to the unrighteous. But thanks be to God who through His Son Jesus has made grace rule over all. Now because of Jesus, God gives us more than our obedience deserves (which appears as filthy rags before Him anyway) and God also redeems the poor choices we make. So we know that we are not just the product of our choices, but a child loved by his or her Father. As important as it is to be obedient to the Word of God (as we see in the following paragraph) at the end of the day, it is only grace through faith in Jesus that allows us to stand as righteous before a Holy King.

As an example of the importance of obedience Samuel said to King Saul in the Old Testament – *"Has the Lord as great delight in burnt offerings and sacrifices, as in obeying the voice of the Lord? Behold, to obey is better than sacrifice, and to heed than the fat of rams. For rebellion is as the sin of witchcraft, and stubbornness is as iniquity and idolatry. Because you have rejected the word of the Lord He also has rejected you from being king."* (1 Samuel 15:21-23).(NKJV) Obedience is a serious issue and has resulted in the rising and falling of many. 1 John 2:3-6 tells us *"We know that we have come to know him if we obey his commands. The man who says, 'I know him,' but does not do what he commands is a liar, and the truth is not in him. But if anyone obeys his word, God's love is truly made complete in him. This is how we know we are in him: Whoever claims to live in him must walk as Jesus did."* (NIV)

We will never be perfect and Jesus was the only perfect sinless human that ever lived so thanks be to God that mercy triumphs over judgment. Our quest is not to be perfect. It is to trust in God and walk according to the Spirit in all that we can. May the grace of God empower you to live your life according to the Golden Rule and forgive, restore and redeem you when you make mistakes.

Lord, thank You for giving me guidelines to live by – not to limit me Lord, but to protect me and bless me. Forgive me for the times I haven't obeyed Your word. Thank You for Your mercy and goodness and the blessings You bestow upon me even when I mess up. Amen.

Day 3: More Blessed To Give (Back) Than To Receive

There are probably a lot better people to share with you about finances than Michelle and me. I also know that there are a lot better resources than this day in our book, but I couldn't really write on sowing and reaping without including the topic of finances. There are more Biblical principles and verses about money than I can even mention in this one short day: verses that talk about giving from your heart and being a cheerful giver; verses that talk about not giving to be seen by men; verses about giving your first and best and so on. After all, Jesus spoke about money more than all other topics in His parables.

One of the lessons, I have learned about money, may not be as commonly taught as others, but it's the lesson about giving back. It's a lesson, I learned from the story of Zaccheus. In Luke 19 you can read about the whole story of Zaccheus. Basically it's a story about a tax collector who was very wealthy. As Jesus was passing by Zaccheus climbed up a tree so he could see better. Jesus saw him up in the tree and asked him to come down so He could go to his house. Zaccheus was so honored and thrilled to have Jesus come to his house that the Bible says "he received Him gladly." In other words he was thrilled beyond belief. Zaccheus was moved so much by Jesus coming to stay with him that he blurted out to the Lord that he was going to give half of his possessions to the poor and he would give back four times as much to anyone he had defrauded. I can just imagine Zaccheus weeping in joy, shouting at the top of his lungs in front of the crowds of people – "Lord this is what I' m going to do!"   As I read this passage of scripture the Lord began to speak to me about people I had cheated in my life.   Please understand I am being very vulnerable, but it is my prayer that as I share my shortcomings with you that you will have the courage and strength to resolve any past shortcomings in your own life.

As I read this story there were three immediate circumstances that the Lord brought to my mind where I had cheated others and they didn' t even know about it.   The first was when I was young. My grandma used to come and watch us kids while my mom and dad went out of town.   On one of these occasions I would go into my grandma' s purse and take a couple of dollars.   I would then ride my bike to the store to buy baseball cards.   When I gathered up the courage to call and apologize to my saintly grandma, who was about 91 at the time I apologized, she was more than gracious about the whole thing and willingly forgave me.   I tried to give her money back, but of course she wouldn' t take it, so I stuffed it in her purse. (shh don' t tell her)

The second instance was a scenario where I had an ATM card that I had recently reprogrammed with a new pin number.   The only issue was that when I got it back, the bank (where my dad worked) had mistakenly encoded my card with my name and my new pin number but with my dad' s account on it.   The first time I took out money and saw my balance I almost fainted.   To a poor college kid it was more than I could handle and I was buying all kinds of stuff: a tennis racket; new shoes; etc. I knew my dad would eventually figure it out so I called and had them switch the information before things got too out of control.   When I called to apologize years later he was very gracious and forgiving, and I gave back the approximate amount that I had stolen.

The last instance the Lord showed me was when I was in Bible school (of all places) and I cheated on one of my Hebrew exams. This was when I was in my internship when God was dealing with me about these issues and I hadn't officially graduated yet. I knew there was a possibility that this would affect my graduation, but the Lord was dealing with me and I knew the right thing was to call the professor. So I nervously called him and told him what I had done and he graciously and willingly forgave me. At a later date the Lord reminded me of something that I had stolen while I was in high school, so I gave back by buying a gift card for that store and then I cut it up.

I don't tell you all this so you will feel burdened about all of your past sins, because the blood of Jesus covers all sin and if we confess our sins God is faithful and just to forgive our sins and cleanse us from all unrighteousness. (1John 1:9) He has removed them from us as far as the East is from the West. At the same time, there may be some hidden sin in your past that the Lord wants to release you from and restore the other person by showing them the honor of apologizing and asking for their forgiveness. I am not saying it is easy. I'm still sitting here sweating as I think about when I confronted these sinful situations. But if the Lord speaks to you about a situation, then you need to resolve it. The Lord will provide the grace and peace and forgiveness that are needed to get through any such situation. When you sow repentance and give back, I believe you will reap an abundance of grace and mercy. So be thankful for the grace that you reap.

The only other concept I wanted to communicate during our day on giving has to do with the law of sowing and reaping. There has been so much focus on what we get from giving and in some cases an overemphasis on the benefit of giving instead of the reason and motive for giving. Now don't get me wrong. I completely understand the concept of sowing and reaping with regard to finances and firmly believe the Word of God and all its promises about reaping bountifully with a good measure and a hundred fold. I believe wholeheartedly the Word of God that says *"he who sows sparingly will also reap sparingly, and he who sows bountifully will also reap bountifully"* (2Cor. 9:6). (NKJV)

But the Bible doesn't say when you will reap it and it is impossible to say how much you will reap for a particular gift, so why make that the focus? It can lead to wrong motives for giving (to get rich) and frustration when the reaping tarries. I think we have all heard stories about God providing miraculous returns with gifts and offerings that have been given. We have a couple of our own. In one instance I lost my job and had just undergone back surgery. In that time of need we sowed a seed of $1,000 in a lady's ministry in New Orleans. She was aware of our situation and she graciously sent us $2,000 back a couple of weeks later. But there have been other times when we gave cars away, which left us with only one vehicle for six months, and we really struggled financially. It wasn't because our faith was any different. There just wasn't an immediate return, but that's ok because we weren't giving to get anyway. So before you give away everything that you have and leave your family with nothing because you've heard that you can't out give God, remember that sometimes sowing seeds of finances is like growing potatoes.

I learned from the movie *Faith Like Potatoes*, based on the life of farmer turned evangelist Angus Buchan, that it takes faith to grow potatoes. The thing about potatoes is that they grow underground, so after you prepare the soil, sow the seeds, pray for rain and weed the ground, you still have no idea if there are actually potatoes growing under the soil. You don't know if there's a harvest until you pull it up. It takes faith to grow potatoes and it takes faith to reap a financial harvest. Sometimes you have no idea what your financial seeds are doing, but you have to have faith that at some point you will reap a harvest. One of the concepts my pastor mentioned a few weeks ago fits well with this point, and that is the more seed you sow, the more seed you have in the ground, and the greater the harvest that will come forth. So keep sowing, keep believing and at the proper time you will reap a harvest. That is one truth that Michelle and I have seen over and over again, reminding us that God is faithful. Time and time again we have seen God come through and provide for us when we had no idea where the provision was going to come from. Food after surgeries, jobs at just the right times, cars when we had no transportation, money for dessert when we couldn't afford it, presents for the kids when we couldn't buy them. Over and over again God has showed Himself faithful in our lives, and I can assure you He is faithful and will be there for you in whatever you're going through. You simply need to trust in Him and call upon His name.

Don't let me discourage you from giving. That is the last thing I want to do. Give your offerings over and above your tithe. Be obedient to what God asks you to give. But give for the right reason and with the right motive. Give cheerfully and give with the right expectations that you will reap a harvest, but you may never know how your harvest is connected with your giving, or when you sowed the seed that produced your current harvest.

Nothing is hidden that will not be made known and nothing is secret that will not be revealed (Luke 8:17). When you give in secret He will reward you openly. God is faithful and He will not disappoint you. So determine in your heart to give back where you have taken, and give out where He leads you. You will find that the generous soul will be made prosperous and he who waters will himself be watered (Proverbs 11:25).

Lord, thank You for your provision in my life, for always meeting my needs. Thank You that You have blessed me to be a blessing. As I sow into the lives of others, emotionally, spiritually and financially, give me patience as I wait for the harvest that will come. Forgive me for the times my heart was not right and I may have taken rather than given, and give me a new motivation to give. Amen.

Day 4: Catch & Release

We had a sermon series at our church entitled "Go Fish" that focused on witnessing and making disciples. So when you read the title, "Catch & Release", don't think I'm talking about a relocation program for panda bears. Most people are familiar with the idea of catching a fish and releasing it back into the water, maybe because it wasn't big enough to keep, or it was the wrong kind or maybe, it winked at you funny. Whatever the reason for releasing fish after you catch them, it is a natural part of fishing.

When God catches (saves) us and brings us into His boat He doesn't immediately cook us and take us to heaven. The normal pattern He uses when He catches us is to bring us into the boat, clean us off, put a wildlife and fishery tag in our heart and release us back into the water. The reason He releases us is so we can lead other fish to the boat, and also because God wants to give us the freedom to swim away. You may ask why God would do that. Why would God catch us, clean us up and tag us just to let us swim away? The answer is because He loves you and He doesn't make anybody stay in the boat. That wouldn't be a relationship that would be entrapment. But God is not like that. He doesn't force Himself on anyone. Once you're in the boat you're His, but He doesn't tie you to a string and trail you behind the boat. He totally releases you to give you the freedom to swim away from the boat. He also gives you the freedom to stay by the boat and receive His protection, His provision, His care and His love. When God puts you back in the water, He will give you instruction. He'll give you tools to help you and He'll even put you in with other fish that will help you stay by the boat. But you don't have to stay. The prodigal son didn't have to stay around the house, and the father probably told him not to go, but he let him go because he loved him and didn't want a robot. He wanted a relationship. The prodigal was always one of the Father's sons. He had just used his freedom to forfeit the provision and protection the Father offered.

Galatians 5:13 says *"for you were called to freedom, brethren; only do not turn your freedom into an opportunity for the flesh, but through love serve one another."* (NASB) It's not a question of whether or not you have freedom; it's a question of what you do with your freedom. You definitely have freedom in Christ. Those whom the Son sets free are free indeed (John 8:36). There is now no condemnation for those who are in Christ Jesus (Romans 8:1). As far as the east is from the west so far has God removed your transgressions from you (Psalm 103:12). There is no sin, no mistake and no past that is left when you are washed clean by the blood of Jesus. Your record has been expunged. Your slate is clean and your guilt and shame are removed. Those who believe in Jesus have been set free from the law of sin and death. Since we know we have freedom as a child of the King, the question becomes what will we do with our freedom? Do we swim as far away as we can so we can barely see the boat and then if the boat moves or if one big wave comes we're in big trouble? Or do we get as close as we can to the boat?

The apostle Paul put it like this – all things are allowable but not all things are profitable (1 Cor. 6:12). When talking about our Christian freedom the question shouldn't be if we **can**, it should be if we **should**. Concerning our Christian liberty there may be things you can do but you shouldn't. If you think by making such a suggestion that I'm trying to limit your freedom I'm not. However,

I am trying to get you to be a good steward of your freedom. Just because there are rules about how to use your freedom, that does not limit your freedom. You are completely free to disobey and you are free to obey. So when Paul said do not use your freedom to indulge the sinful nature but use it to serve one another in love, (Gal. 5:13) he wasn't taking away your Christian freedom. He was liberating you to use your freedom to serve God and not yourself.

Being thankful for our Christian freedom means understanding what Paul is writing about to the Galatians in Chapter 5. Paul gives us four instructions for being thankful for our freedom and being good stewards of it. The first instruction comes from chapter 5 verse 1. *"It was for freedom that Christ set us free; therefore keep standing firm and do not be subject again to a yoke of slavery."* (NASB) The first thing is to understand your freedom and to know that no amount of religious rituals, good works or lack of sin can make you right with God. This was a huge deal in the Galatian church. They were taught by legalists that you had to be circumcised to be right with God, so Paul goes on a tangent for verses 2-12 explaining this one point that Christ has truly set you free and you don't have to do anything like being circumcised or perform religious acts to belong to Christ. It's not about your prayers. It's not about your confessions. It's not about your giving and it's not about your suffering – it's about having faith in Jesus.

The second instruction that Paul gives about freedom is what we've already discussed in verse 13. *"Do not indulge your sinful flesh or use your freedom to satisfy your sinful nature."* This is the opposite of Paul's first instruction, in which he talks about the extreme of trying to use external measures to determine internal righteousness. Basically, that we fake our righteousness by trying to do things externally that can never make us righteous internally. In the second instruction Paul talks about the opposite extreme where we ignore our righteousness and indulge ourselves with the things of this world that we want to make us happy. Basically, we forget righteousness. Paul was writing to the Galatians because they had been deceived by legalists into believing you had to be circumcised in order to be saved. That's why he spent eleven verses expounding on his comment about freedom from the chains of slavery. But if Paul was writing to the church today he might have a different emphasis. We must never lose sight of the freedom that we have in Christ. And yet at the same time we can't allow our freedom to become an excuse to live in sin.

If Paul was writing to the church today he might say, "O foolish Galatians! Who has bewitched you that you should not obey the truth and that you allow the love of the world to penetrate the walls of the church. Your fathers forget their children. Your mothers commit adultery. Your elders chase after wealth. You ignore the orphans and the widows. Practicing homosexuality is accepted and pornography is rampant even in the church. Was there no price paid for your freedom? Was there no blood shed and was there no death that was paid? If yes, then why do you trample over the name of Jesus like a doormat instead of esteeming Him above the mantle? The death He died was free for you but it cost Him everything, so why do you cheapen His sacrifice by disgracing His bride, the church, in the name of freedom? Wouldn't it have been better to remain poor? Wouldn't it have been better to be unhappy and unfulfilled in this life than to defame the name of Jesus in the world by breaking His commandments and teaching others to do the same? But thanks be to God who says that where sin abounds, grace abounds even more. And that because of the faithful remnant that has cried out for revival – God is sending a purification to His church. Then there will be no confusion between light and darkness and each man will have the chance to see the truth and follow it, because it is the truth that will set you free." I'm probably way off, but maybe it would sound like that.

The third instruction Paul gives us concerning Christian freedom comes from the second half of verse 13 and talks about what we should be doing with our liberty. "*...Do not use liberty as an opportunity for the flesh, but through love serve one another.*" Instead of indulging the sinful flesh, we are to be using our liberty through love to serve one another. To put it another way, instead of asking how far away can I get and still be part of the school (family), the question should be how close can I stay to the boat and still serve others. That is what we are supposed to be doing with our freedom, serving one another. Jesus came to this earth not to be served but to serve. If there was anyone who ever had the right and freedom to pick up his sticks and go home it was Jesus. But Jesus did not use His freedom to get disgusted and quit or sin in any way. Instead He became the greatest servant of all.

That is what our freedom is for – to serve. You don't *have* to serve. You don't *have* to stay by the boat and serve Christ's bride. You are free not to serve. There is no obligation and no contract and certainly no influence on your eternal relationship with Jesus based on whether you serve or not. But God's way is the best way. Those are His instructions in His word for us and for our benefit. When you sow service for God's kingdom, you reap temporal and eternal benefits, as Jesus said when the disciples were fighting about who was the greatest in Luke 22:26-29. "*But not so among you; on the contrary, he who is greatest among you, let him be as the younger, and he who governs as he who serves. For who is greater, he who sits at the table, or he who serves? Is it not he who sits at the table? Yet I am among you as the One who serves. But you are those who have continued with Me in My trials. And I bestow upon you a kingdom, just as My Father bestowed one upon Me.*" (NKJV) Notice what Jesus said they would reap for their service in these verses. Jesus said He would give them a kingdom! If you will stay close to the boat and sow service in this life, you will reap in this life and eternally in the next.

The instruction Paul ends with seems to summarize the entire discussion of Christian freedom, if not the whole Christian existence, in verse 16. "*I say then walk in the Spirit, and you shall not fulfill the lust of the flesh.*" (NKJV) Paul then goes on to show what it looks like when we fulfill the lust of the flesh and what it looks like when we walk in the Spirit, as he defines the fruits of the Spirit for the very first time. In verse 25 Paul summarizes the entire chapter by saying, "*since we live by the Spirit, let us keep in step with the Spirit.*" (NIV) I've never been in band but I've always appreciated and been fascinated by marching bands. The unison of the music and their motion is certainly entertaining. I've never really seen someone out of line or going in a direction other than what was dictated by the conductor, but I'm sure it happens. As Christians, we're not supposed to march to the beat of our own drum, we're supposed to follow the conductor. We are to walk according to the Spirit. If you have marched to the beat of a different drummer or if you have used your freedom to swim away from the boat take this opportunity to repent and to go God's way instead of your way. Repent – turn around and march God's way and serve. Use your freedom to follow God and to serve His purposes and not your own. Recognize your freedom to march in a different direction than the boat – but use your freedom to serve others and to walk in the Spirit because you are thankful for your freedom.

Lord Jesus, thank You for loving me enough to "catch" me and then "release" me, giving me the opportunity to follow You, serve others and walk in unison with You through the leading of the Holy Spirit. I repent for the times that I have gone my own way. Thank You for the freedom I have in You. Lord, help me to use that freedom for Your purposes and not for my own. Amen.

Day 5: Rest In Peace

Although rest in peace is probably the most common inscription on tomb stones, it is really a message that we need to hear while we're living not after we're dead. After we're dead there will be peace in heaven and there won't be peace in hell. But while we're alive, resting in peace is something we should certainly be thankful for. With all the hustle and bustle of today's world – stress, anxiety, worry, sleeplessness and even panic attacks- there is a great need for us to rest in peace on earth as it is in heaven.

You can imagine with four young children in the house that in the natural there is a lot of commotion, but in the spiritual there is a great sense of peace that fills our home. One of the reasons for that is because of the authority my wife and I exercise in our home. Something I have learned being in the restaurant and retail business that is always fast paced, is that it is important to exercise authority in those types of environments. The more chaotic the environment, the more authority is required. Notice I didn't say to exercise anger. There have been times in the past that I have yelled and become angry only to regret it later. But an important concept to remember is to exercise your authority and not your anger. It is important to maintain order, to follow the rules and to be in control, but not at the expense of exploding in anger. When you are the person in authority there are consequences that can be implemented, and discipline that can be exercised so there is no need to lose your peace, just exercise your authority.

Peace is something that is tested when challenges or adversities arise. That's why a good acronym for PEACE is Peaceful

Even After Challenging Events. When things don't go your way, or when the unexpected arises or when challenges come against you, that is when your peace is tested. Like when Jesus was asleep on the boat in the storm, or when there wasn't enough food to feed 5000 people, or even when the soldiers came to arrest Him to take Him to His death. In each of these scenarios the disciples worried and fretted but Jesus held His peace. He was Peaceful Even After Challenging Events. We need to be thankful for peace in our own lives because we'll be more content, more joyful and more fulfilled when we're at peace. But most importantly when we stay at peace even in the face of challenging events, we give God the opportunity to shine forth with His glory. We give God the opportunity to stop the storm, to miraculously provide and to work all things together for good to them that love Him.

There is no use fretting, or complaining or getting upset when challenges arise. I know it is easier said than done, but when we are at peace God can move and show His glory. As my pastor taught recently, when one door closes another one opens. God is never late. Even when it looks hopeless - trust in God, ask Him to fill you with His peace and see things from His perspective. When Lazarus was sick, Jesus didn't fret or run to his side to heal him. In fact, by the time He got there, Lazarus had been dead four days. But God is never late. Instead of healing him, He raised him from the dead. When we trust in God and His ways, He will show Himself strong in our lives. When you're praying for something and it doesn't happen, don't fret. Instead, look for another door, another way or an alternate route God may want you to take. When you come to a dead end, it doesn't do any good to curse the dead end. It's only helpful to regroup, re-evaluate and move in a new direction.

The church I go to is in the process of starting a new campus in the city of New Orleans, and in preparation for starting the church we've been having free food events for the community with gifts for the kids like school supplies or basketballs. At the most recent event there was such a great turn out of people from the community that there wasn't going to be enough food for the volunteers. This is something we have had challenges with in the past, and the leadership team for the event has tried to make sure that those who serve are blessed in their serving and have adequate refreshments. It became apparent that with such a great turn out that the food lines never really ended and there wasn't going to be a way to get food to the volunteer tent. I communicated the bad news to the lady in charge of the volunteer tent and she was very peaceful about the situation. A few minutes later, one of the other workers came up and said she was going to go to the closest fast food restaurant and get a bunch of burgers for the volunteers. I believe that because the lady at the volunteer tent held her peace, God provided in another way. It wasn't what was planned, but God still provided and came through in a miraculous way.

That's why the <u>Serenity Prayer</u> is so powerful. *God grant me the serenity to accept the things I cannot change; courage to change the things I can; and wisdom to know the difference. Living one day at a time; Enjoying one moment at a time; Accepting hardships as the pathway to peace; Taking, as He did, this sinful world as it is, not as I would have it; Trusting that He will make all things right if I surrender to His Will; That I may be reasonably happy in this life and supremely happy with Him Forever in the next. Amen.* Through this prayer we understand that there are circumstances beyond our control and it doesn't do any good to become anxious or nervous about them. The only good that we can do is to realize that we do not have any control in that situation and in response turn to God who made the heavens and the earth. When we turn to God with the situations **we can't change** that helps us to keep our peace and gives Him the chance to show up and change the things only **He can change**.

There are some ways to try and influence your external circumstances more than others. For instance, setting boundaries is very important for trying to maintain peace in your life. We talked about this in one of the small groups I'm in at the church. We all agreed there are seasons each of us go through that are going to require more time in one area of our lives than others. After you're married you should spend a lot of time with your spouse and adjust to living with a partner. When you have a child there is a lot of time you will have to spend caring for the new little one. When you start a new job or have seasonal projects there will be an increased amount of time that needs to be spent in that area of your life.

This is something we need to continually evaluate so that our lives do not get out of balance. Imagine that the priorities in your life are a circle split up into sections or pie pieces. At the center of the pie is a circle that has God in the middle. Whatever life stage you are in, that circle should never disappear, but as you grow in your walk with God your time with God will grow. But your other areas will fluctuate. For instance, if in your life you have a pie piece for church, wife, kids, work, and recreation, we must continually be evaluating what our priorities are and if we should be spending less time in one area and more in another. As I already indicated, there will be times in your life that require more time than others, but it shouldn't become a permanent imbalance. If you're putting in lots of hours for tax season, there should be an adjustment after tax season. If you've been doing a lot of volunteer work at church helping with a large project, then you may need to adjust after the project is complete. At the same time, if you're spending all your time with your family but aren't providing for their needs, you will need to adjust your priorities. We all go through changes in life, but we need to make sure we are being intentional with our time instead of just letting the wind blow us where it will. Of course, the most important time is the time you spend with God at the center of your circle, and then He will help you determine priorities and set appropriate boundaries in your life. Ultimately, when your life gets out of balance in a particular area that you can't change, you will have to give it to God and let Him handle it.

Whatever it is, God can handle it. Whatever it is, God can take it. Whatever it is, God can do it. If you are feeling heavy burdened or that the weight you're carrying is too much, then remember that God said His yoke is easy and His burden is light. *"For unto us a Child is born, unto us a Son is given; and the government will be upon His shoulders. And His name will be called Wonderful, Counselor, Mighty God, Everlasting Father, Prince of Peace. Of the increase of His government and peace there will be no end"* (Isaiah 9:6-7a). (NKJV) There is no end to the authority and peace of Jesus. There is no circumstance, no challenge and no opposition that is too great for Jesus. There is no end to His peace. Our peace will never be perfect, but Jesus' is. We must choose to aim for excellence and not for perfection. Excellence in all that we do and in all that we are, but there was and is only one who will ever be perfect – Jesus.

Jesus, thank You for Your peace in my life. Thank You that I can cast my anxieties and burdens upon You and rest in the assurance that You are in control of all things. Jesus help me to remember that during the storms of life that You are in the boat. Amen.

Day 6: REWARD

Everyone has seen REWARD signs for lost dogs, turning in criminals or for other lost items. But one of my favorite verses in the Bible has the promise of a reward. In Hebrews 11:6 it says, *"And without faith it is impossible to please God, because anyone who comes to Him must believe that He exists and that He rewards those who earnestly seek Him."* (NIV) You don't have to have talent to seek God. You don't have to be rich, you don't have to be pretty, and you don't have to have a master's degree in theology. God rewards all those who diligently seek Him – big and small – short and tall. God's word is true and if you diligently seek Him you will receive a reward.

I remember when I was at a church conference in Los Angeles. One of the nights I felt very strongly that the Lord had said He was going to show up that night. I told other people and I was believing He was going to physically manifest Himself in a glory cloud or something. After the speaking engagement for the night there was a powerful time of worship and the presence of God was awesome. In fact, I spent most of the time face down on the ground worshipping God. Eventually the music stopped, the worship ended and the people left, but I was disappointed because I hadn't "seen" God. I continued to press in to God and decided since they were kicking everyone out of the auditorium I was going to go outside in the walkway surrounding the event center and worship God. By this time almost everyone had gone and as the students left the building I continued worshipping. The only other person I saw was a woman that was singing and dancing to the Lord around the walkway as well.

As the last people left the building, I sat down in some bleachers outside the auditorium feeling disappointed. It had been a great night and a powerful time of worship, but somehow I was dejected because God didn't show up how I had expected Him to. As I sat there and the last group of students left the building all of a sudden someone showed up and asked how I was doing and if he could sit with me. He was very tall and his eyes were so big and inviting, my immediate thought was that he was an angel. I asked him what his name was and what school he was from, and after he answered my questions I sort of resolved that he wasn't an angel. Then as he sat down he put his arm around me and asked what was bothering me. I told him I had expected God to show up and he said, "Well, it says that wherever two or three are gathered together, there He is with them."
I told him he was right, but I had expected God to show up physically. He asked me if I had any other questions. I said no and he told me to keep seeking God every day. And then he was gone. Was he an angel? I don't know – if he was I could kick myself for not asking more questions but I don't know for sure. The point he left me with - whether he was an angel or not, has never left me and that is to seek God every day. Seek Him in the morning. Seek Him in the evening. Seek Him on the earth. Seek Him in His mighty heavens. Seek His face all you who call upon the Lord that He may reveal himself to you in new and powerful ways.

One of the things my dad taught me growing up is that there will always be someone more talented, and there will always be someone smarter than you, but one thing that you can control is how hard you work, and you can always work harder than anyone else. My dad taught me to be a hard worker and for that I am grateful. The same principal applies to seeking God. There may be other people who are smarter or able to memorize more Bible verses or pray more eloquent prayers or have been saved all of their life or are from the greatest spiritual heritage. But you alone control how diligently you seek God. There are very few external factors that influence your ability to diligently seek God. It is a matter of your will, something that you can control and a decision that you alone can make. Your parents can' t seek God for you. Your spouse can' t seek God for you and your pastor can' t seek God for you. You must seek the Lord yourself, and if you sow seeking you will reap rewards.

Some of the ways we can seek the Lord are through fasting, prayer, worship and through His Word. There are other spiritual disciplines as well, but these are the primary ways I have implemented in my life to seek the Lord. I remember one time when I was fasting. One of my friends in the church I was in at that time found out about it and he asked me how I had gotten hooked on fasting since it wasn' t very common in that church. I told him I didn' t really know, but it was in the Bible so I wanted to do it. There are whole books on fasting that can give you a lot more and better information, but I have fasted from all kinds of things. I' ve had water only fasts, no meat or sweets fasts, bread and water fasts, liquid only fasts, fruit and vegetable fasts. I know to some of you it sounds more like a diet plan, which has probably been an added benefit in my life, but the purpose has been to seek God, not to lose weight.

There are lots of reasons to fast - to seek God, to hear His voice and seek direction, to pray for breakthrough, to offer a sacrifice of praise. Most of the time I have tried to keep the fasting under wraps so as not to be seen by men. I have been on fasts for between a day and 40 days, but most have been between three days and a week. One of the most miraculous responses to one of my fasts was when I was on a 21 day fast. We were in Tennessee seeking direction about what to do and where to go after the "door had shut" where we were at. I think it started as a fruit and vegetable fast and then the last couple days I did water only, but the type or tradition of the fast is not important. It is the spirit of the fast that God desires. As it says in Isaiah 58 it is not the fast that God desires but the sanctified life that results from the fast. That's why it's so important when you fast for Lent, or any other time not to do it because it's tradition in your church or in your family, but to specifically seek God, do His will and have faith for God to answer your prayers during your fast. It is not the act of the fast that brings results, it is faith in the God of the fast who answers your prayers.

Back to the 21 day fast in Tennessee. We were at the end of our rope, unsure what to do, where to go and we were seeking God's direction. We had just built a beautiful new home and we had to leave the church we were at. Our prayer was for God to speak to us His will no matter where or what it may be. After about the first week of the fast, my wife and I began to hear in our hearts about going to New Orleans. At that time we had never been to New Orleans and didn't even know anybody who lived there. But God was making it sufficiently clear to both my wife and me about going to New Orleans. By the end of the fast we would be together and would hear something about New Orleans, and just look at each other and laugh, it was so obvious. We heard it on a TV show, we heard it in a pastor's message at church, we heard it on the radio and we had relatives that were traveling there for the Women's Final Four. It was very clear. Needless to say we made it to the New Orleans area and are still seeking God about His ultimate plan for us here.

Most of my fasts have not been that immediately clear. Often God speaks or moves after the fast or in the natural I don't see any movement and believe for a future harvest in the spirit. The point is that fasting is like sowing and reaping in any other arena, the reaping may be immediate or delayed, but those who diligently seek the Lord will receive a reward.

Since I have been saved, I have always enjoyed praying and spending time talking to God, and praying for others as well. One of the most intense seasons of prayer I had was after hurricane Katrina struck. We had come back to the New Orleans area and I had to take a job delivering papers in order to supplement our income while I worked at a major retail store. It was really a great way to pray because I would get the paper, review it quickly, and start praying as I bagged the newspapers about anything that God would impress on my heart that day. Then I would continue to pray and worship God as I delivered the newspapers in the neighborhood. I know that I prayed a lot of prayers and I can't tell you which ones were answered, but I know they were heard. I remember praying for people to come and help in New Orleans – physically, spiritually and financially. I remember praying for godly businesses to come to New Orleans. I remember praying for the churches, the schools, the police and for the righteousness of the political system. I know that God heard my prayers, but what affect they had I have no idea. But that is not the point because I know God rewards those who diligently seek Him. Seek God in your prayer life. Seek Him in the morning. Seek Him at the noon time. Seek Him in the evening. When you diligently seek the Lord through prayer you will receive a reward.

Another way to seek the Lord is through worship. I love to worship the Lord even though I can't sing very well. One of my favorite things to do is to get worship DVDs and sing along with them. We also have the Christian music channel on our TV, and when I'm not working I enjoy going to concerts, conferences and prayer meetings or even worshipping the Lord together as a family in our home. One of the most recent seasons of my life has been spent with an extended time of worship after I would get home late from work. I work nights and no one else is awake when I get home. I've had to learn to shut Michelle's bedroom door so that I don't wake her up, but I've found during this season, God has been granting me favor and victory in my life. Worship has served as a buffer against the enemy. God has also supplied me with revelation and inspiration during this time. It has been a reward for spending time with Him in worship and He will reward your worship as well.

Seeking God through His Word has been very fruitful and beneficial for me as well. *"The grass withers, the flower fades, but the word of our God stands forever"* (Is. 40:8). (NASB) So if it is possible for you to memorize scripture, there is great benefit in learning the Word of God and carrying it with you in your heart wherever you go. Even if it's a few short verses to begin with, God will reward your effort to seek Him. You can write verses down and repeat them over and over again, or simply memorize from your Bible as you pace throughout the house, or you can listen to Bible recordings and continue to play certain sections of scripture over and over. At some time or another I have implemented all of these tactics to learn God's Holy Word. I could do a lot better at scripture memorization, but because of what I have learned there have been times when the Lord brought scriptures to mind to help someone else or to encourage them through prayer.

One of the most powerful times that God used His Word to demonstrate His power through my life was when I was at a prayer retreat with pastors. I spent three days fasting and meditating on God's Word and secluding myself from outward influences of life like radio and TV. I remember just playing recordings of scripture over and over, listening and meditating on the Word of God. During one of the prayer sessions I began to pray and the Spirit of God came upon me so strongly that I became unaware of what I was saying or what was going on around me. When I became aware again, there were about 12-15 of the pastors standing around me interceding as the Word of God came forth from my mouth. To this day I still don't know what I said during that prayer. Obviously this is not the type of thing that happens every day, and most of us don't have the time or opportunity to spend that much intense time with God's Word. In fact, most of the supernatural things that God does in our lives come through our normal day to day interactions with those whom God places in our path. But if you will take the time to seek God through His Word then He will reward you.

Just as with financial giving the reaping of the reward is not the motive, it is simply the result. The motive is to seek God and when you seek God you will find that God is no respecter of persons and His reward is for all those who will call upon His name. Seek Him today. Seek Him forever. *"Hear, O Lord, when I cry with my voice, and be gracious to me and answer me. When you said, 'Seek My face,' my heart said to You, 'Your face, O Lord, I shall seek'"* (Psalm 27:7-8). (NASB) *"Ask, and it will be given to you; seek, and you will find; knock, and it will be opened to you."* (Matt. 7:7). (NASB)

Lord, as I seek You each and every day, help me to be thankful for the rewards I gain from that. As I read Your word, help it become real to me and give me direction in my life. As I worship, help me to feel Your presence and receive Your joy. As I pray, help me to hear Your voice. As I fast and seek You, help me to know Your plans for my life. Thank You that I can seek You in so many ways and You are there waiting for me. Amen.

Complete & Reflect On Weekly Activity

WEEK 5

GIVING THANKS

FOR eTernity

Day 1: Introduction & By Grace You Have Been Saved

God doesn' t owe you a thing. If you could see one concept differently, it would change your life forever. This world is not your home. Your citizenship is in heaven. It' s a matter of perspective. Colossians 3:1-4 says, "*Since, then, you have been raised with Christ, set your hearts on things above, where Christ is seated at the right hand of God. Set your minds on things above, not on earthly things. For you died, and your life is now hidden with Christ in God. When Christ, who is your life, appears, then you also will appear with him in glory.*" (NIV)

It' s like a village in the Amazon jungle that was trying to figure out why every time it rained their village flooded. They tried to dig a moat. They tried irrigation. They tried to build levees, but nothing seemed to work. One day one of the villagers decided to climb to the top of the nearby mountain range and lo and behold he saw a large waterfall and lake just miles from the village. This lake was contributing to their village being flooded every time it rained. The villagers had tried everything they could to stop the flooding, but they didn' t have the right perspective. That is how understanding that heaven is your home opens your eyes to your circumstances in this life. Set your minds on things above, not on earthly things. When you do, you' ll see that God matters more and stuff matters less. You' ll see that this life is fading but heaven is eternal. You' ll see that other people matter to God more than what you get in life. That is why I say that God doesn' t owe you a thing. He gives you everything, but He owes you nothing. In Him you live and move and have your being, and every good and perfect gift comes from above, but none of it is owed to you. Even though He doesn't owe it to you and you don't deserve it, He gives it to you anyway because He is a good God. God is a good Father, not some dead beat dad that abuses, leaves or ignores. When we recognize that God doesn't owe it to us, we are much more thankful because it's by His grace that He provides for us and sustains us. Therefore, we can be thankful for our life now and for eternity because we don't deserve any of it.

Being a citizen of heaven is like living inside a game show where the bonus round comes before the main part of the game. The goal of the game is to win. You win by believing in Jesus and going home to heaven. The majority of your prizes and time will be spent in the heaven part of the game. But in this game of life the bonus round comes first and any prize you get here on earth is just a bonus. If you simply spend all your time collecting bonus points and don't learn how to win the game, you will ultimately lose. But if your main focus is to win the game by believing in Jesus and collecting prizes that you will get in heaven, then everything else you get here on earth is just a bonus. Some of us have more bonuses than others, but at the end of the game it won't be your bonuses that matter. It will only matter whether you won or lost, and what kind of prizes you'll get if you've won in heaven. Do you want your prizes here on earth or for eternity in heaven?

Tell them what they've won Johnnie – "Thanks for playing today's game. You've racked up lots of bonus prizes during your time in the game, but unfortunately you didn't win." Or "Congratulations, you've won the game and you get to spend eternity with God. You don't get to keep the bonus prizes you won, but because you played the game so well, your prizes in your new home include a mansion decorated in the finest Italian leather, as well as your dream job assignment and a life long supply of your favorite foods and goodies. But that's not all, Jesus himself is coming to visit you in 3 weeks and He has a message for you – Well done good and faithful servant. And He is bringing a present with Him that will blow your mind."

The people in Hebrews understood what it meant to play in the game. Hebrews 11:13-16 *"All these died in faith, without receiving the promises, but having seen them and having welcomed them from a distance, and having confessed that they were strangers and exiles on the earth. For those who say such things make it clear that they are seeking a country of their own. And indeed if they had been thinking of that country from which they went out, they would have had opportunity to return. But as it is, they desire a better country, that is, a heavenly one. Therefore God is not ashamed to be called their God; for He has prepared a city for them."* (NASB)

Setting your sights on heaven at times means taking your eyes off of earthly things so you can more effectively focus on what's eternal. To help us take our eyes off of earthly things, your activity for this week is fasting. Although my preference is to fast from foods, I will let you decide what you are going to sacrifice. Some people choose to fast from all solid foods; others will eat only fruits and vegetables. Some people fast from television. Whatever you choose, the objective is to take your focus off of that earthly pleasure and focus instead on Christ. In addition, as you fast I'm asking you to seek the Lord with all your heart and study about eternity. Spend time in prayer and in your Bible researching what eternity will be like, and believe that God will give you new revelation about living for eternity. Have you ever thought about the fact that you won't ever have to fast in heaven? You won't have to fight against your sinful

flesh. You won't have to fast so that you can hear God better –
He'll be right there. And you won't have to fast to focus on God
more or believe for breakthrough. Once you're in – you're in.
But in the mean time, in the here and now, there are thoughts to
capture, demons to fight, breakthroughs to possess and truths to be
heard. Seek God this week and watch Him stir your soul in a new
way.

*For many walk, of whom I have told you often, and now tell
you even weeping, that they are the enemies of the cross of Christ;
whose end is destruction, whose god is their belly, and whose glory is
in their shame—who set their mind on earthly things. For our
citizenship is in heaven, from which we also eagerly wait for the
Savior, the Lord Jesus Christ, who will transform our lowly body that
it may be conformed to His glorious body, according to the working
by which He is able even to subdue all things to Himself.* (Philippians
3:18-21) (NKJV)

By Grace You Have Been Saved

Let me get right to the point. The only way that you can be thankful
for eternity in eternity is to have a relationship with Jesus. He died
for you so that your sins could be forgiven, and He rose again to
defeat death so you could live forever in heavenly peace. I can't
promise you that if you accept Jesus as your Lord and Savior, you
won't have any more struggles or challenges. I can't promise you
that you will be immediately healed of a disease, or that you will
strike it rich even though God does want you to prosper and be in
good health. What I can promise you is that you can *know that you
know that you know* when you die that you will go to heaven and live

forever in eternal bliss. If you know Jesus as your Lord and Savior you will have peace and joy, and the emptiness that leaves you feeling alone, worthless and keeps you up at night will be replaced with the peace that passes all understanding, the hope of eternal life and the joy of the Lord. There is no substitute for the presence of Jesus in your life. No drug, no material possession, no position, no degree and no person can fill the void in your life that was meant to be filled by God. So wherever you are and whatever else you may be doing right now besides reading this book, take a few seconds and say these few things to God.

"I'm sorry for all of the things that I've done wrong. Please forgive me. Thank you for sending your Son Jesus to die on the cross and rise again from the grave to grant me forgiveness. Please come into my heart and take over my life. I surrender to your will and your ways. Amen."

That's it. It's that easy. It's easy, but it wasn't cheap. It cost Jesus His life so that you could say that prayer and live forever with Him in heaven. Thank him for your new life and for eternity.

There is no one beyond the grace of God. Everyone who calls upon the name of the Lord shall be saved (Acts 2:21) – there's just something about that name. Jesus is the name above every name. Every knee will bow and every tongue will confess that Jesus is Lord (Phil. 2:10-11). The only difference is that some will call him Lord in **this** life, but **all** will eventually call Him Lord. It's His name that saves. It's His name that heals. His name is above every name. It's above the name of every disease. It's above the name of every disorder. It's above the name of every addiction. It's above the name of every phobia. All authority in heaven and earth has been given to the man by the name of Jesus. Call upon His name today and confess that His name is above whatever name has got you down so that the power of God can be released in your life to overcome your challenges. Jesus your name is greater than the name of poverty. Jesus your name is greater than the name of failure. Jesus your name is greater than the name of confusion. Jesus your name is above every name and you are above every circumstance in my life.

Luke 19:10 tells us that Jesus, came to seek and save those who are lost. That was His purpose in coming to this earth, to seek and to save us, for we were all lost. The heart of our Savior is for us – we are the reason He came. The heart of Jesus is for you. He came to this earth, suffered and died for you. If you were the only one here on earth, He would have still come, for you. Heaven rejoices over one sinner who repents. Think about the six billion people in this world. The Bible says that heaven rejoices when **one** comes to salvation. That is a big deal and a major event to have a party in heaven over one person out of six billion. In fact, it's kind of outrageous. It would be like a billion dollar company throwing a company picnic every time they saved a dollar. On the surface it doesn't really seem to make sense that God would go to all that trouble for just one person unless of course every person meant that much to God.

Some of you may be wondering why you're doing what you're doing in your life, or why you're where you are. But if there's anyone where you are who doesn't believe in Jesus, they are at least one reason. God cares so much for lost people that He would send you to a new job or a new location just for one person. Do not underestimate the power of one. God said that He would leave the 99 just for the one. Ultimately, the goal is fully committed followers of God, but before anyone can be a disciple they must be a believer. Billy Graham is only one person. Mother Theresa was only one person. Be faithful to reach the one or ones in your life wherever you are. Do not wait for a platform or a ministry or the perfect opportunity. Be faithful with the mission God has given you today and you can help cause a party in heaven.

Being thankful for salvation means really understanding the concept of forgiveness. Jesus described it best when He went to a Pharisee's house and there was a prostitute there that was crying and wiping Jesus feet with her tears and hair. The Pharisee thought this was disgraceful but Jesus used these circumstances to tell a parable about forgiveness. He asked if there were two people who owed money to a credit card company, one who owed $3500 and the other owed $35,000, which one would be more thankful if both the debts were forgiven. Obviously the one who was forgiven the greater debt would be more thankful. The actions and love that the prostitute was showing toward Jesus was motivated by the great degree of her forgiveness. The Pharisee, however, did not show any great favor toward Jesus because he didn't recognize his own need for forgiveness.

So we see that the key to being more thankful for your forgiveness and salvation is to recognize your need for that forgiveness. Not that we want to encourage sin or poor behavior so that we can be more thankful for our forgiveness. The key is not to sin more but to recognize it more. The key is to recognize that no matter how good we have been or how long we have been saved – even if it's been since you were a child - our sin has been great in the eyes of God. In fact, if there is anyone in your life that has offended you – and there may even be people that come to mind - we have offended God more than that person ever thought about offending us. Maybe someone has betrayed you – you have betrayed Jesus; maybe someone has ignored you – you have ignored Jesus; maybe someone has forgotten you – you have forgotten Jesus;

maybe someone has hurt you – your sins nailed Him to the cross. The more we recognize our sin and our need for Jesus, the more thankful we will be for His forgiveness and salvation.

The more thankful you are for your salvation and the more you see God's grace in your own life, the more likely you'll be to share that gift with someone else. You share what you appreciate. One of the things my pastor talks about that helps you to be thankful for your salvation is to remember what it was like the day before you were saved. How depressed, how empty, how meaningless that life felt, but that was all before you surrendered your life to Christ. Now you can celebrate. Now you can be confident. Now you can be thankful. You talk about what you're thankful for. You share what's meaningful to you. As you focus on God and His undeserved goodness toward you – you'll grow in your desire to tell others about Him because of your feelings of appreciation and gratefulness. Tell your neighbor, tell your friends, tell your coworkers, tell the world how thankful you are that Jesus died for you.

Father, thank You for sending Your Son to die on the cross for me. Thank You for forgiving me and making me a new creation. Jesus, thank You for paying such an enormous price for me. I love You. Amen.

Begin & Review Weekly Activity

Day 2: Baptized With Fire

Job Description: Wanted – Person with supernatural ability to change circumstances for the better, help bring peace to the anxious, confidence to those in doubt and to comfort those in need.   Also wanted is someone that can influence others actions so that those around them are more loving, kind, and gentle but at the same time has enough power to fend off negative ideas and forces so that others can be the best that they can be. Living conditions will be deplorable with stinky, sweaty situations and you will often be met with opposition to your suggestions, leading and direction. Your pay will be negligible and your only reward will be the lives you change who become growing mature disciples that love God and thank you for your assistance.   Experience with healing, miracles and words of wisdom preferred.

Of course the only person that would fit that job description, at least on a permanent basis, is the Holy Spirit. He is God and He is a distinct and separate person of the Trinity, and unfortunately forgotten, overlooked and taken for granted. Although this week is entitled eTernity, it is in the here and now that we are directed and guided by the Holy Spirit and how we respond to Him will determine our eternal destination. If we reject the Holy Spirit and the gift of God's Son Jesus, then we will spend our eternity away from God in hell. But if we accept God's gracious gift, then the rest of our lives are spent with the Holy Spirit who lives inside of us and who leads us to eternity in heaven.

Of the many and various works the Holy Spirit performs in the world, there are two primary works we should be thankful for. The first is often referred to as the fruits of the Spirit as told in Galatians 5: love, joy, peace, patience, kindness, goodness, faithfulness, gentleness and self-control. These fruits are primarily for our own benefit and everyone receives the seeds of these fruits when we accept Jesus as our Savior. Through these fruits the Holy Spirit provides us with the resources necessary to help us effectively maneuver through this life. For example, the fruit of love provides the emotional ability we need to be in positive relationships with other people. These fruits can also positively affect others. As we are loving and kind and gentle, others receive the fruit of our actions. But the primary function of the fruits of the Holy Spirit is for our own benefit and our own well being. If we aren't bearing the fruits of the Spirit the consequences are often painful and detrimental in our own lives. We should be thankful for the fruits of the Holy Spirit because they are for our good and our benefit.

When we take these things for granted we are not only forgetting to thank the Holy Spirit who lives inside of us, we are neglecting the very fruits that He has given us to protect us from our sinful nature. Often we can see when others are not bearing the fruits of the Spirit. But what we fail to consider is that when we don't bear them ourselves, we are opening ourselves up to negative situations and consequences. When we're not peaceful we can be filled with stress, worry and anxiety which can lead to health challenges. When we're not being self-controlled we can make bad decisions that negatively affect us. When we're not loving, we miss out on the emotional bonds that we so need and desire. Conversely, the more loving we are the more positive relationships we'll have. The more joyful we are the more influence we'll have. The more peaceful we are the more health we'll have and so on. The fruits of the Spirit are given to us by the Holy Spirit to help us live in the fullness of all that God has for us.

As soon as you accept Jesus as your Lord and Savior the Holy Spirit dwells inside of you – bam you have the seeds of the fruits of the Spirit. It's a package deal. You get saved, you have the seeds and the degree to which you walk in the Spirit and deny the sinful nature will determine your ability to bear the fruits of the Spirit. As Jesus said, *"Abide in Me, and I in you. As the branch cannot bear fruit of itself, unless it abides in the vine, neither can you, unless you abide in Me"* (John15:4). (NKJV) So although you cannot bear fruit without the Holy Spirit who dwells inside of you – once you are saved you can pick any one of the fruits of the Spirit and say I want to work on being more kind today because it is a seed that you already possess.

The second work of the Spirit we need to be thankful for is known as the gifts of the Spirit. Unlike the fruits of the Spirit which are all deposited in our hearts upon salvation the gifts of the Spirit are just that, they are gifts. The Bible says that the gifts of the Spirit are the work of one and the same Sprit, and He gives them to each one, just as He determines (1Cor.12:11). The Holy Spirit is the giver of the gifts and He determines which gifts you get. The Bible tells us to pray for spiritual gifts and to earnestly desire the greater gifts, but at the end of the day you can't make the Holy Spirit give you gifts – that wouldn't be a gift. At the same time, the way you steward that gift may determine your effectiveness and growth in that gift. But you can't just pick a gift and say, "I want this one today." You get what you get, be thankful for it. That doesn't mean we can't pray for more gifts and earnestly desire the greater gifts, but we need to start by saying thank you for the gifts the Holy Spirit has already given us. Don't let your primary focus be on the gifts, let it be on the giver – the Holy Spirit and your relationship with Him. One of the books that has really helped me in my relationship with the Holy Spirit is <u>Good Morning Holy Spirit</u> by Benny Hinn. For some of you the whole idea of gifts of the Spirit may be a new concept and you might be thinking, "If I can have a gift, how do I get it?" It's simple, really. The same way you get any gift – you ask. You don't command or demand or politely hint, you simply ask. Ask the Holy Spirit to fill you with His presence and He will. *"If a son asks for bread from any father among you, will he give him a stone? Or if he asks for a fish, will he give him a serpent instead of a fish? If you then, being evil, know how to give good gifts to your children, how much more will your heavenly Father give the Holy Spirit to those who ask Him!"* (Luke 11:11,13). (NKJV) Ask Him for His presence – ask Him for His gifts and let Him bring you whatever He determines and then be thankful for it. Thank Him for His presence in your life. Thank Him for His gifts in your life.

As you receive the gifts of the Holy Spirit you will realize very quickly that His gifts are not for you, they are for others. Where the fruits are primarily for you and for your benefit, the gifts of the Spirit are primarily for others. Yes, you get to enjoy them and use them and demonstrate them, but the purpose of the gift is not to be consumed, it is to be distributed. As far as the gifts of the Spirit are concerned, you are the middle man passing on the "product" to the consumer. You simply warehouse the gifts holding them for the people that need them. The Holy Spirit is the manufacturer of the gifts and He distributes them to you. You warehouse the gifts and then distribute them to the end user. For instance, one of the gifts in 1 Corinthians 12 is healing. God is the author of all healing. God as the manufacturer takes the gift of healing and through the Holy Spirit distributes it to you. You are the warehouse for the gift of healing. It wouldn' t do much good for you to just walk around with the gift of healing in your warehouse and never distribute it. That would be like collecting cars that you never drive and putting them into your garage. People may come over and look at what' s in your warehouse and they might even be impressed, but what good are they doing anybody? The gifts of the Holy Spirit are not for us, they are for others for the common good. When we realize that the gifts of the Holy Spirit are not for us then God can work in miraculous ways through us, as we use the gifts that He has given us to help others.

As the gifts of the Holy Spirit are used and demonstrated in your life, you will learn the important principle of being filled with God. As John the Baptist said in John 3:30, *"He must increase, but I must decrease."* (NKJV) The fuller we are of the Holy Spirit the less full of ourselves we will be and the more God can use our gifts. The key with using your gifts or for defeating sin in your life is not to try harder it is to allow God to increase in your life so that you may decrease. Put simply - don' t try harder – yield better. This involves dying to self and surrendering your ways for God' s ways. When you take up the cross and surrender your ways, your agenda, your will, your dreams, your plans – you make room for God' s ways. Death to your man made ways makes room for the presence of the Holy Spirit to come and fill up your life. It is the surrendered and yielded life that God can most effectively use. As you sacrifice, as you surrender and as you put others first, you make room for God to fill you with His presence and bless others with His gifts.

I recently had the opportunity to go on a mission trip to Oaxaca, Mexico. I have always had a heart for missions and was very excited to be a part of this trip that would travel to unreached villages delivering the gospel. Just weeks after I was to take my trip, my wife and daughter would be traveling to Belize for a mission trip working with children. They were just as excited as I was, but the reality of us needing $5,700 for both trips meant tons of fundraising. We all began our fundraising and believed in faith God would provide our funds. Within weeks of our trips, it became clear to me that God was asking me to make a sacrifice with my trip. Michelle and Kaley had raised almost $3400, but still needed $600 to reach their goal. I had raised $600, and felt that God was asking me not to go this year, but instead to give the money I had raised to Michelle and Kaley so they would meet their goal and be able to go. God had indicated that it was not my time, it was Michelle's time. I had to surrender what I really wanted in order for God to fulfill the purpose He had for them. In doing that, they were blessed, I was blessed to see how excited and happy they were, and tons of lives were changed in Belize! It was a tremendous blessing for me, my wife, my daughter and the people of Belize because I yielded to the Holy Spirit instead of trying harder.

As you grow in your relationship with the Holy Spirit and as you become more and more thankful for His presence in your life, there are a few quick things that you should know about Him. First, God sent the Holy Spirit to earth to help you. *"But the Counselor, the Holy Spirit, whom the Father will send in my name, will teach you all things and will remind you of everything I have said to you"* (John 14:26). (NIV)

Second, if you believe in Jesus the Holy Spirit dwells inside of you. *"Therefore I tell you that no one who is speaking by the Spirit of God says, 'Jesus be cursed,' and no one can say, 'Jesus is Lord,' except by the Holy Spirit"* (1Cor. 12:3).(NIV)

Third, you can be filled with the Holy Spirit. *"Do not get drunk on wine, which leads to debauchery. Instead, be filled with the Spirit"* (Eph. 5:18).(NIV)

And finally, you can know the presence of the Holy Spirit in your own life. The Holy Spirit is as unique as the people He inhabits but His presence can be known none the less. Sometimes it may be in the form of tears that overwhelm you or it may be tingling down your spine, or laughter that overcomes you or His sweet small voice that you hear in your heart. However He expresses himself to you, know that you can be filled with His presence and He is there with you. Even as you read these words right now believe that His presence is filling your life in new and powerful ways.

Father, thank You for giving me the Holy Spirit to live inside of me, to strengthen me and to guide me. Come Holy Spirit and fill me with your power that enables me to shine the light of Christ as I maneuver through this life. Thank You for Your fruit and for Your gifts and trusting me to share those gifts with others. Use me Lord, fill me Holy Spirit. Amen.

Day 3: Every Word That Comes From The Mouth Of God

The Word of God is living and active and sharper than any double edged sword able to judge the thoughts and attitudes of the heart (Heb. 4:12). The Word of God is just that. It is truly God's Word to His people. There is nothing magical or mystical about the Word of God. It is from God and that is enough.   It is the incorruptible, unchangeable, inspired word of God. Have you ever thought about how it's possible that the Bible written between 2000 and 4000 years ago still has practical advice for our lives today in the 21st century? Having trouble with your finances? The answers are in the Word of God. Need help raising your children? It's in the Word of God. Need help with your marriage? It's in the Word of God. You need to understand your wife better? (ok so almost all the answers are in there!) But seriously, whatever your need, God already knew it and put it in His message to His people.

In America it's easy for us to take the Word of God for granted. There is a Bible in almost every home. There are family Bibles lying on coffee tables all across this country and there is a Bible in almost every hotel dresser drawer. What a blessing to have such immediate access to God's Holy Word whenever and wherever we need it. The only problem is that because it has become so accessible, it has become underused, unappreciated and even unauthoritative for some. If only we knew what some people had to go through in other countries just to get a Bible – fasting, praying, and believing for years to get their hands on just one Bible in their language. Some have risked their lives just for the opportunity to get to know the God that created them and to read the message He left for them, and others have died trying.

So how is it that our Bibles grow dusty and our reading of them is neglected or mundane? How can we regain passion and desire to hear from the Lord Himself? After all, the grass withers and the flowers fade but the Word of God endures forever. I am all for marketing Bibles and different translations of Bibles and making Bibles more accessible, understandable and useable. But if it's at the expense of not appreciating what God has so carefully preserved for us throughout time, then maybe it's time to get back to the Bible. Colossians 3:16-17 says, *"Let the word of Christ richly dwell within you, with all wisdom teaching and admonishing one another with psalms and hymns and spiritual songs, singing with thankfulness in your hearts to God. Whatever you do in word or deed, do all in the name of the Lord Jesus, giving thanks through Him to God the Father."* (NASB) We see two important truths about God's word in this passage. The first being that we are to let the word of Christ richly dwell within us. We can't do that if our Bibles just sit on our coffee tables or if we have the best designer Bible known to man but don't know what's on the inside. The only way that the Word of Christ is going to richly dwell in us is to read it, meditate on it, memorize it and inwardly digest it. As it says in Deuteronomy 6, *"These words which I am commanding you today, shall be on your heart. You shall teach them diligently to your sons and shall talk of them when you sit in your house and when you walk by the way and when you lie down and when you rise up."* (NASB)

The other truth of God's word that we see in Colossians 3 is that whatever we do we are to give thanks. This includes the things of God. In fact I would argue that *most importantly* we should give thanks for the things of God. Although this final section of the book is about the things of God, it is the most important section to be thankful for because it is the only part that is going to matter for eternity.

We need to be thankful for the Word of God. We need to thank God that He cared enough to give us His Word for our instruction, for His promises and to get to know Him better. We need to be thankful that He didn't give up when the Israelites worshipped that golden calf and Moses broke the ten commandment tablets. He made another set and He gave us another chance. We need to be thankful for inspired writers that God used throughout history to faithfully complete the work that God had given them. We need to be thankful for the scribes and writers of the manuscripts that painstakingly copied every word of the Bible letter by letter before there were copy machines. We need to be thankful for the Jews and Christians that defended copies of Scripture with their very lives during times of persecution and war. We need to be thankful for the disciples who memorized and orally repeated the stories of Jesus. We need to be thankful for the contemporary translations of the Bible in the languages of the people. We need to be thankful for the opportunity to sit and dine with God and Him with us – to hear Him speak to us, to tell us He loves us and that He's pleased with us.

One of the rewards for appreciating the Word of God is that we will have it at our fingertips whenever we need it. If we are thankful for the Word of God and we meditate on it and memorize it, then whenever we need it – it will be there for us. In Ephesians 6 we find that the Word of God is the sword of the Spirit. It is the only offensive weapon that is described in the armor of God. It only makes sense then that if we want to be on the offensive – if we want to plunder the treasures of darkness and if we want to expand the kingdom of God - then we need to carry the sword of the Spirit with us.

My little boy Josiah just saw the Chronicles of Narnia movie Prince Caspian and there is quite a bit of sword fighting in the movie. In the fashion of a true boy, he picked up a plastic stick and carried it around with him for the next two days everywhere he went. He even asked if he could take it to bed with him and mom caved and let him have his "sword" in bed. Then I was up late that night and I heard some commotion and walked down the hall to find Josiah standing in the hallway half asleep, but he still had his sword. He had gotten up to go to the bathroom and didn't even really know what he was doing, but he still had his sword.

If you will meditate on the Word of God and memorize it and inwardly digest it, then you will have it at your disposal whenever you need it. You may be half asleep or under duress or going through a tough time, but you will have your sword of the Spirit to fight against your fear, your sin, your depression, your challenges and the enemy. God's word will encourage you, it will bring victory over your circumstances and it will supernaturally change your perspectives. God's word will bring faith; it will emotionally heal you and give you wisdom to draw upon.

Reading, meditating and learning the word of God is only half the battle though. As G.I. Joe says, "knowing is half the battle," but the other half is doing something about it. As the Bible itself says we must not just be hearers of the word only but doers as well (James 1:22). And in Psalm 119:11 it says *"Your word I have hidden in my heart, that I might not sin against you."* (NKJV) There is a purpose behind learning God's word and that purpose is doing what it says. In Matthew 7 we see that there are two ways to handle God's word. One is foolish and one is wise. The foolish way is to learn and read, talk about, do Bible studies and even memorize the Word of God but not do anything about it. That is the way that eventually leads to destruction and pain. The wise way is to learn and read, talk about, do Bible studies and even memorize the word of God and then do what it says. The Bible says when you handle God's word the wise way by obeying it and doing what it says, then when the winds of change or the storms of life come, you won't be destroyed. Notice it doesn't say that the same storms won't affect you or happen in your life, but when they do you will be protected because you obey the Word of God and do what it says.

Reading God's word is a tradition in some of our families. We read it after dinner because that's what grandpa always did. We read it at bed time because that's how dad would read us our bed time stories. Tradition is good in some ways. God is the author and creator of tradition. He commanded the Israelites to incorporate traditions into their lives to help them remember who God was and what He had done for them. Whether it was feasts He instituted or commands about remembering His word – God instituted those traditions.

We have good traditions in our own lives as we celebrate anniversaries and birthdays and give thanks to God for our time on this earth. We celebrate the Christian holidays of Christmas and Easter. However, it is not the tradition that God desires, but the heart of the tradition – the condition of our heart that remembers Him and gives Him thanks for His provision and His presence. Romans 15:4 says "*For whatever things were written before were written for our learning, that we through the patience and comfort of the Scriptures might have hope.*" (NKJV)

Unfortunately, everything that God institutes the devil tries to pervert, and traditions that were instituted to remember and fellowship with God can become meaningless repetition that defame the name of God. Our approach to the Word of God has this same choice of attitude: to be the greatest joy in our lives that is filled with vigor and excitement as we get to know God all over again, or to be a burden as we drudgingly open our Bibles for the millionth time because we have to. Give thanks for the Word of God. Appreciate its life, its newness, its relevance, its depth, its detail and its mystery. It's God's love note, His instruction manual, His history book, His promises, His story about how we win, His journal, and His Word for you and for your life. Open His Word and fall in love with Him over and over again.

Lord, thank You for Your word. It is a lamp unto my feet and a light unto my path. As I read and meditate on Your word, help it to become alive to me in a way as never before. Forgive me for the times I've taken Your word for granted. Speak to me Lord as I search Your word. Amen.

Day 4: As It Is In Heaven

I don' t know about you, but at times I struggle with even imagining what heaven will be like. I know that there will be streets of gold and gates made of pearls and walls made from your birthstones as is described in Revelation 21. But what does the perfect blade of grass look like and what does the perfect air smell like and what does the perfect day feel like? I think that no matter what heaven looks or feels like the first thing that we will think when we get there is – wow I wish I would have invited more people! It is going to be more beautiful, more peaceful and more fulfilling than any of us can imagine.

There are some misconceptions about heaven that make it less than an exciting prospect for some and may even make it difficult for some to be thankful for one of the greatest of all God' s gifts for us. Some people have visions of sitting around, bored out of their minds, eating grapes all day. Some people think it is going to be incredibly monotonous worshipping Jesus all day every day. Well you' re half right. We will be worshipping Jesus all day every day, but what you may fail to understand is that it' s not boring or monotonous. In fact, everything we do can be worship to the Lord. When we have a heart of thanksgiving and worship toward the Lord, our chores are worship, our work is worship, our time with family and friends is worship, our recreation is worship, and our worship is worship. You won' t be up in heaven bored out of your gourd (whatever that means). It will be the most exciting, invigorating, creative place you could ever imagine. Our contentment will be perfect, our peace will be perfect, our joy will be complete and we will be lacking nothing.

If you think you are going to get to heaven and be disappointed, then you are greatly mistaken. God has good plans for you to prosper you and not to harm you. Think about the Israelites and their venture into the Promised Land. God told them they would eat fruit they had not planted and enjoy possessions they had not earned. It was a land flowing with milk and honey. It was a land of abundance like they had never seen before with clusters of grapes so big that they could hardly carry them. How much more abundant and plentiful will our eternal dwelling place be! Just as it takes faith to believe in Jesus, there is an element of faith that is required to believe in heaven. If the Bible told us everything about every little detail of heaven it would be a no brainer and no element of faith would be required. Yet God gave us enough information to know that we don't want to miss it.

The most comforting thought about heaven is that God will be there. The Bible tells us there will be no need for the sun or moon because God will be there and His glory will be so great that it will fill heaven. I don't know about you, but wherever the glory of God is – that's where I want to be, to be in His presence, filled with His love, overcome by His peace and surprised by His joy. *Lord, I want to know you more. I want to see your glory. Even if I cannot look upon your face, then pass by for I know that even the hem of your robe fills the temple with your glory. Lord, I want to be where you are. I would rather be a doorkeeper in your presence than to dwell in the house of the wicked. One day in your house is better than a thousand days elsewhere. Oh to dwell in your presence is like laying on a bed of rose pedals, or to feel the sweet breeze of the ocean on the shore, or the warmth of the sun that beats against my face or to sit on the porch and to enjoy the summer rain these things are but a foretaste of the feast that is to come. For the glory of the Lord is beyond understanding and the greatness of the Lord is indescribable.*

Another great thing about heaven is that Jesus said in John 14, He was going to prepare a place for all who believe in Him. That's right, you're probably going to get your own place in heaven. And if I know anything about my loving Father it's going to be awesome - decorated just the way you like it before you even get there – your very own mansion in the sky. My mansion is going to be made of stone with a circle drive and a long winding sidewalk welcoming all who approach. There will be plenty of greenery with beautiful blooming trees with flowers. The side of my mansion that faces the glory of God will be completely translucent so that His glory will fill the house. The inside will be colorful and spacious with beautiful paintings and designs that tastefully fill the room each one with their own unique story telling of God's goodness. The carpet will be a plush Berber and the granite of the kitchen will run onto the enclosed patio with the in ground pool that is halfway inside and halfway outside. There will be a beautiful stone waterfall that pours into the outside section of the pool on one side and into a small pond with tropical fish and coral on the other side which leads to a larger body of water where my pet dolphin can swim and return when I call him. Hey, it's my mansion! You can have a dog if you want, but I want a dolphin. I don't want a mansion on earth. I want a mansion in heaven because in heaven I'm sure it will always stay clean. What will your mansion look like?

Another thing that we learn about heaven from the Bible is that there will be treasures there. In Luke 12:31 and following we find an overarching principle that our primary concern is to be directed toward the kingdom of God, doing God's will with our resources and not storing up things for ourselves. Jesus said, *"But seek the kingdom of God, and all these things shall be added to you. Do not fear, little flock, for it is your Father's good pleasure to give you the kingdom. Sell what you have and give alms; provide yourselves money bags which do not grow old, a treasure in the heavens that does not fail, where no thief approaches nor moth destroys. For where your treasure is there your heart will be also."* (NKJV) One of the coolest things about your treasures in heaven is that they will be there waiting for you when you get there. They can't be lost. They can't be stolen and they can't be washed away by a hurricane or swallowed up by an earthquake. When you get to heaven all the treasures you've stored up for yourself will be waiting there for you. So every time you give money for an offering, or care for the orphan, or visit the imprisoned, or pray for someone or tell someone about Jesus, or encourage a friend in the Lord - you are storing up treasures in heaven. It's not selfish to expect treasures in heaven. It is a truth of God's word that they will be there waiting for you.

The other truth we see about heaven from the Bible is that we will have responsibilities in heaven. This is evident from the parables of the minas and the talents in Luke 19 and Matthew 25. It only makes sense really. Think about it. In the perfect Garden of Eden Adam had responsibilities and work that was assigned to him, but it was only after the fall that it became toilsome and painful. So naturally in perfect heaven God will make all things new and the original intention of work and responsibility will be restored. God will use stewards in heaven just as He uses stewards on earth. We will just be taking care of different stuff and in heaven there won't be any days that you wake up and don't feel like doing it. In heaven you will find great fulfillment and satisfaction in the responsibilities that you have – every day without exception. I can't tell you what the jobs will be, but I can tell you that if you are faithful with what God gives you on earth, you will receive more in heaven. It will be better and more fulfilling than your perfect dream job. You may have a job on earth that is boring, meaningless, frustrating and doesn't pay what you'd like. Be faithful in it because in heaven your job will be based on your stewardship on earth, not on your talent, accomplishments or family name. Everyone may not have the same type or level of job on earth, but the test is the same – are you faithful with what you have?

Another important fact about heaven is that it is forever. In fact, everyone will live forever, it is just a matter of where. One of the places in the Bible that makes this quite clear is in Luke 16. It is the story of a rich man who had a large estate, fine clothes, and fine food. There was also a poor man named Lazarus (different from the Lazarus that was raised from the dead) and he sat at the rich man's gates begging for food and hoping for scraps from the rich man's table. He had sores on his body and he was so weak that animals would come and lick his sores. It happened that both of the men died and Lazarus went to heaven, but the rich man went to hell. The rich man was able to see Lazarus in heaven comfortable and well and sitting by Abraham. The rich man begged Abraham to let Lazarus come and give him just a drop of water because of his great agony in the fires of hell. But Abraham told him that it was impossible because of the great separation between heaven and hell. We see that heaven is an eternal dwelling place. Once you get there you can't lose your spot and neither sin nor evil will ever be able to enter in. It is forever. It is eternal. You only get one shot at your life here on earth and your posture on earth will determine your position forever. For every man is appointed to die once.

We need to know that heaven is our true home and we need to be excited to go. In fact we want to go – not that we would ever do anything to cut short our time to love and disciple others – but we know that heaven is our home and to die is gain for us as Christians. We need to be thankful – so thankful that we are ready at any moment to leave this world behind to go onto our final resting place. Ready to leave our possessions, ready to leave our positions and even ready to leave our relationships for the eternal bliss that awaits us in heaven. By now you are plenty excited about going to heaven with your new mansion and your new job and we haven't even talked about the food!

Finally, in addition to being excited we need to be ready. In Matthew 25 there is a parable that you may be familiar with about 10 bridesmaids that were invited to a wedding. It was night so all ten had lamps. Five of the bridesmaids didn't fill up their lamps with oil and when they had to wait for the wedding to start, they went back to get more oil. But when they did the groom came and started the wedding banquet. While they were gone the door closed and they missed the wedding. So it will be when the Son of Man is revealed – they ate, they drank, they bought, they sold, they planted and they built. Jesus could come back at any time to take us to heaven and we need to be ready. We need to be ready to stand before God and answer to Him about why we should get into heaven – because of Jesus. We need to be ready to tell others about how wonderful heaven is going to be. And we need to be faithful with whatever God gives us. We need to be about our Father's business not just our business so that when the door opens we will enter into His joy.

Father, thank You for giving me a new perspective on how amazing heaven will be. Help me to live my life storing up my treasure in Heaven and waiting eagerly for the time we are united in our eternal home. Thank You for loving me enough to not only make my life on earth incredible, but to give me the hope of an eternity that's mind boggling. I love You Lord. Amen

Day 5: Let There Be Light

When God spoke the world into existence He said, "Let there be...." and there was. God's creation is so vast, so amazing, so inspiring and so complete. Isn't it interesting to think about the fact that there have been people who have prayed for others to be healed, and there are some who have even raised people from the dead, like Paul in Acts 20:11-12. But never has there been anyone who created something out of nothing except for God. Even some of the greatest inventors in history like Edison and Franklin never created anything. They just discovered how something worked – God had already created it. Or maybe you're thinking about artists who have "created" something like Picasso or Michael Angelo. But still you have to admit that if God created them, then their very work was not a creation, but a discovery of what God had put inside of them. God is the only one who has created something out of nothing.

What a job He did. Not only does His creation function like clockwork, there was just the perfect amount of oxygen and carbon dioxide in the atmosphere; the tide of the moon perfectly pulls the oceans in and out; the weight of the earth perfectly maintains our gravity; and the distance of the sun perfectly warms our planet without blowing it up. Truly, it is amazing and breathtaking as well. Just the thought of watching the sun set over the water, or seeing the trees up north in their autumn beauty, or the majestic mountain tops that fill the sky warms my heart. God's creation truly is majestic. Think about the seven wonders of the natural world. Although there is not complete agreement about what 7 wonders are included in the list, these seem to be the consensus: Grand Canyon, North America;

Northern Lights, North America; Mount Everest, Asia; Paricutin Volcano, South America; Harbour at Rio de Janeiro; Victoria Falls, Africa; and the Great Barrier Reef, Oceania. The only one of these I have seen is the Northern Lights. I remember travelling in Michigan to go up north for the weekend to my uncle's cabin and there was a huge traffic jam. It lasted for what seemed like hours. The only good thing was that the Northern Lights could be seen filling up the sky with their brilliance and majesty. I was with my wife and my future brother in law and if I would have known that I was looking at one of the seven wonders of the natural world, I probably would have appreciated it more, but it was amazing. I think the traffic jam was probably just God saying, "Hey, stop and look at my creation here, this is good stuff!"

What part of creation do you enjoy the most? Is it the beach, the countryside, the mountains or the thick forest? Part of the reason for God's creation is your enjoyment. Maybe it is the park by your house, or the golf course, or the land at your hunting camp or the beach. What part of God's creation are you especially thankful for? I love rainbows and sunsets and the beach and the water. Even though you can't swim in the water where I live, there is something beautiful about it. I love to go to zoos and aquariums and see all the different types of animals and species in God's creation. His imagination is endless and His creativity is infinite.

Take the Grand Canyon for starters. It is so huge and its majesty and beauty is unimaginable. It encompasses 1,218,375 acres which represents 1,904 square miles. The Grand Canyon is about 18 miles across at its widest point and the deepest area is about 3 miles below the canyon rim. God must have a sense of humor with the flat billed platypus, the long nosed aardvark and the hammerhead shark. One of God's most majestic creations I have always appreciated is the hummingbird. When I was young and we lived in Michigan, my family and I would go up north to my uncle' s cottage and on occasion, we would visit my grandma' s brother who lived nearby. When we went to their house out in the country, they always had humming bird feeders that attracted all kinds of these birds. It always amazed me that their wings would move so fast that you couldn' t see them. They would remain stationary in the air with what seemed like very little effort, but you knew that their wings were moving a million miles an hour. In fact, a hummingbird' s wings move at 53 wing beats per second! Their wings beat 53 times by the time you finished reading this sentence! God is so amazing and how glorious is His creation!

Have you ever thought about how complex and precise God' s creation is? The human eye alone is enough to amaze and perplex. *The human eye is a very complicated system consisting of the delicate conjunction of some 40 separate components. Let us consider just one of these components: for example, the lens. We do not usually realize it, but the item that enables us to see things clearly is the constant automatic focusing of the lens. If you wish, you can carry out a small experiment on this subject: Hold your index finger up in the air. Then look at the tip of your finger, then at the wall behind it. Every time you look from your finger to the wall you will feel an adjustment. This adjustment is made by small muscles around the lens. Every time we look at something, these muscles go into action and enable us to see what we are looking at clearly by changing the thickness of the lens and turning it at the right angle to the light. The lens carries out this adjustment every second of our lives, and makes no mistakes. Photographers make the same adjustments in their cameras by hand, and sometimes have to struggle for quite some time to get the right focus. Within the last 10 to 15 years, modern technology has produced cameras which focus automatically, but no camera can focus as quickly and as well as the eye.*

For an eye to be able to see, the 40 or so basic components which make it up need to be present at the same time and work together perfectly. The lens is only one of these. If all the other components, such as the cornea, iris, pupil, retina, and eye muscles, are all present and functioning properly, but just the eyelid is missing, then the eye will shortly incur serious damage and cease to carry out its function. In the same way, if all the subsystems exist but tear production ceases, then the eye will dry up and go blind within a few hours (http://www.darwinismrefuted.com). As you can see the eye is one of the most complex parts of the human body and we usually don't even give it a second thought. We open our eyes and we see form, color, depth, texture and all of it without even thinking about it or even trying. God is so amazing and His creation is indescribable. How unsearchable are His ways.

Have you ever as a kid lied on your back, looked up into space and counted the stars in complete amazement at the beautiful arrangement God provided? *On a clear, moonless night about 3,000 stars are visible with the unaided eye. A small telescope will increase the number to around 100,000 stars. But this is just the beginning! The stars we can easily see are all in our corner of the Milky Way Galaxy. The entire galaxy numbers about 100 billion stars. And beyond the Milky Way are other galaxies with many shapes and sizes. Around 100 billion such galaxies are known to exist.*

Taking the Milky Way as an average galaxy, the total number of known stars is thus (100 billion)^2=(10^{11})^2=10^{22}. These estimated stars number 10,000,000,000,000,000,000,000, when we write this number out. This figure would be pronounced as "ten billion *trillion" stars. Suppose these stars were divided up among the world's total population of 6 billion people. Then each person on Earth would receive more than 1 trillion stars! Yet all these stars may be only one page in God's catalog of the heavens. New instruments continue to probe deeper into space, with no end in sight. What an excellent way for the Creator to show his glory! Whatever the number he has created, God calls all the stars by name, and he keeps count of them (Ps. 147:4; Isa. 40:26) (www.christiananswers.net).* God calls the stars by name and they number in the trillions. How much more does He know your name and every fiber of your being?

God knew you before you were in your mother's womb. You were created by the same God who made the stars and the humming bird and He's even more proud of you. You are the crown of His creation. You are God's masterpiece. He made you just a little lower than the angels. I know that there is a tremendous amount of attention paid toward outward appearance in our day, but God is pleased with how you look, just like you are. You are God's creation, He knew how He was going to make you and He likes you just the way you are. Yes we should be good stewards of our bodies because they are temples of the Holy Spirit, but there has been such a focus on outward appearance that we have forgotten that God doesn't look at outward appearances – He looks at the heart. Just as I tell my three sweet little girls all the time – you look beautiful, but it's how you look on the inside that matters the most. *"Charm is deceitful and beauty is passing, but a woman who fears the Lord, she shall be praised"* (Proverbs 31:30). (NKJV)

There is a tremendous amount of pressure for girls especially, but also for guys to live up to the swimsuit models and TV superstars standards of appearance. But God says *"bodily exercise profits a little, but godliness is profitable for all things, having promise of the*

life that now is and of that which is to come." (I Timothy 4:8). (NKJV)
Part of being thankful for God's creation is being thankful for how
He made you. Before being saved I used to want to get a nose job
because I have a big nose. But I came to realize that God loved me for
me. There is such a preoccupation today with looks and perfection
we forget that we get new bodies when we get to heaven anyway.
Why make a temporal investment in improving your body that will
die with you instead of investing in your soul? I'm not saying that
there is something necessarily wrong with getting liposuction or a
nose job or other plastic surgeries, but at the end of the day we still
need to understand that God loves us for us. Scripture does not
condemn physical beauty or say that our outward appearance is
insignificant, but God doesn't consider physical stature. He
considers the stature of your heart. God made us and He's going to
take us back without a second thought about how we look – the only
part of our body that He is looking at is our heart. As the song
<u>Everything Glorious</u> by the David Crowder Band states, "You make
everything glorious and I am Yours so what does that make me?"

From the song of a bird to the roar of a lion, from the
delicateness of a butterfly to the expanse of the Grand Canyon,
God's handiwork is evident. God created the heavens and the earth
to fill the formless and empty darkness (Genesis 1:2). He created man
and woman in His image because He desired relationship with us.
God created everything and everyone for a reason. After His creation
God said, "It is good." Take a moment to be truly thankful for this
amazing place God created, not only for His enjoyment but ours as
well. Then when you think it can't get any better, remember God's
creation is eternal. Some day there will be a new heaven and a new
earth that's better than we can imagine. "Lord of all creation, of
water earth and sky, the heavens are your Tabernacle, Glory to the

Lord on high. God of wonders beyond our galaxy, You are Holy, Holy. The universe declares your Majesty and You are Holy, Holy, Lord of Heaven and Earth" (God of Wonders, by Third Day).

Lord, thank You for the beauty of Your creation. Creation truly does sing Your praises and shows Your majesty. What an amazing place You've allowed me to live and enjoy while here on earth! You are holy Lord! Amen.

Day 6: The Gates Of Hell
Will Not Overcome It

The church may change but it will never cease. It may be underground or over ground, official or unofficial, in a house or a cathedral, but the devil will never stop it. Jesus said in Matthew 16:18 that He will build His church and the gates of hell will not prevail against it. However, as we see in Ephesians 6:12, we are engaged in a battle against the spiritual forces of evil for we do not fight against flesh and blood. Satan is real and will do all in his power to try and overcome the church. However, God is not worried and we shouldn't be either. *"The God of peace will soon crush Satan under your feet"* (Romans 16:20a-b).(NASB) *"Behold, I give you the authority to trample on serpents and scorpions, and over all the power of the enemy, and nothing shall by any means hurt you"* (Luke 10:19). (NKJV)

God is not intimidated or even concerned. In fact when Satan rose up against God, God didn't even lift a finger. In Revelation 12 we see that God sent the archangel Michael and the angels to handle Satan and he was cast down to the earth. When Michael contended with Satan for Moses' body in Jude 9, he called upon God's help and said. "The Lord rebuke you." But when Satan challenged God, God didn't lift a finger – He didn't have to. It wasn't even a contest. If it was a serious threat, then you figure God would have gotten involved. But He didn't need to. He said Michael you go handle it. God is not surprised by any scheme of Satan nor is He worried. God is in control. He knew what was coming and He had a plan for it. So when Jesus said that He will build His church and the gates of hell will not prevail against it, He wasn't just trying to sound powerful or important. He was declaring a promise that He could keep, that no matter what happened or how hard Satan schemed and tried, he was not going to be able to destroy the church. For those of you ESPN fans, you'll appreciate my illustration from Sportscenter. (Sorry ladies, some of you will have no idea what I'm talking about here so I apologize in advance). On ESPN's Sportscenter they have had a saying in the past that when someone was playing really well that he was unstoppable. They call it "en fuego" (on fire) and then they would say "you can't stop him you can only hope to contain him." That is like the church. It is "en fuego" (with the Holy Spirit) and the devil can't stop it – he can only hope to contain it.

One of the primary ways that Satan tries to contain the church is by dividing it and by separating its intended unity. Ephesians 4:5 tells us we are to be unified: *"One Lord, one faith, one baptism; one God and Father of all, who is above all, and through all, and in you all."* (NKJV) I am not so idealistic to think that there is no need for different denominations or groups of Christians because after all, God created the church and He made it up of many members. *"For as the body is one and has many members, but all the members of that one body, being many, are one body, so also is Christ. For by one Spirit we were all baptized into one body—whether Jews or Greeks, whether slaves or free—and have all been made to drink into one Spirit. For in fact the body is not one member but many."* (1 Corinthians 12:12-14).(NKJV) Although there were no denominations when Paul wrote this, his point remains that there are different groups of people, but we are all one in Christ. There are many different denominations, but there is only one body – the Church and there is only one head – Jesus. Understanding that brings unity. And unity brings power and victory to the church. Remember, however, Satan is using all he's got to attack our unity. Psalm 133 tells us *"Behold, how good and how pleasant it is for brethren to dwell together in unity."* (NKJV) When brothers live together in unity there the Lord bestows His blessing.

One day I noticed Satan's scheme to try and separate my wife and me as we were going through some financial difficulties. We had one vehicle that was unusable because of some pretty extensive repairs that needed to be done and we didn't have the money to fix it. I started fault finding and criticizing my wife for all the reasons that we didn't have enough money. She was very negative making statements like we're going to lose our van and there is no way we're going to make the payment. The point is that both of us were wrong and we were really pushing each other's buttons to how we were responding to this financial pressure. Remember Ephesians 6:12? *"For our struggle is not against flesh and blood, but against the rulers, against the powers, against the world forces of this darkness, against the spiritual forces of wickedness in the heavenly places."* (NASB) Thankfully God got our attention with what the enemy was trying to do by dividing us and getting us to blame each other instead of giving each other the benefit of the doubt and encouraging each other. Instead of fighting with one another we should have been united in facing our common challenge.

In the past the church has fallen prey to the schemes of the enemy in similar ways. Instead of uniting and fighting against the spiritual forces of evil, we are fault finding, blame placing and competing with each other. Our judgmental thinking and hypocritical actions prevent us from overcoming and keep us limited in our effectiveness in the earth. But it is time to recognize the scheme of the enemy to keep us fighting with each other instead of against him and stop the destructive cycle. I am not suggesting that we should naively forget our differences or doctrines and all hold hands and sing Kumbaya, but we should make every effort to unite against the enemy of our souls. I recognize that this is more easily said than done, but the effectiveness of the church and the fate of cities and countries are hanging in the balance. It will take sacrifice, deference, forgiveness, understanding and compassion, but it is worth it all in order to plunder the treasures of darkness. And just as my wife and I were able to become closer as a couple by recognizing our need for unity, the church may find that the greatest blessing may come in being united with one another, even more than the victory that results from it.

The secret of the church is the people – the assembly – the ecclesia. There is power in unity and in gathering together. Jesus said wherever two or three are gathered in His name there He is with them (Matthew 18:20). I have talked to Christians before who don't have a church home because of preference or offenses or whatever the case may be. But the Bible says, do not give up gathering together as some are in the habit of doing (Heb. 10:25). I'm not saying that going to church saves you anymore than being in a barn makes you a horse, but there is a reason God wants us to be a part of a larger body of believers. Not only does it provide us with fellowship and support, but God's effectiveness and power is multiplied in the context of the church.

When believers are gathered together in unity in the name of Jesus, their effectiveness is multiplied by the power of God. It's like playing tug of war by yourself or with others. The more people that are on your side of the rope, the greater load you can pull and the greater effectiveness you are going to have. You can't pull very much by yourself no matter how strong you are, but as you add people to the team and you' re pulling as a unified group, your ability multiplies exponentially. That is why when Jesus sent the disciples out He sent them out two by two. It wasn' t just for fellowship or protection it was for maximum effectiveness in His kingdom. There is a multiplication of God' s power when people are gathered together for the cause of Christ. So be thankful for your church, and if you don' t have a regular church that you attend, find one and join together with your pastor and the other believers in the great tug of war.

The church is as important to God as a wife is to her husband. The church is called the bride of Christ. Ephesians 5:25 says, *"Husbands, love your wives, just as Christ also loved the church and gave Himself for her, that He might sanctify and cleanse her with the washing of water by the word, that He might present her to Himself a glorious church, not having spot or wrinkle or any such thing, but that she should be holy and without blemish."* (NKJV) God cares about the church. He cares about every little child. He cares about every widow and He cares about everyone that feels abandoned and alone. God loves His church because it is made up of His people. God will defend His church. God will promote His church. God will discipline His church. And God will bless His church. God loves His church so much that He sacrificed His only Son so that you would even have the chance to be a part of it, and He is moving on the earth to purify and glorify His people in the church so that it will be holy and without blemish. God' s church is described as *"the household of God, which is the church of the living God, the pillar and support of the truth"* (1 Timothy 3:15). (NASB) God will see to it that His church is protected.

When we first moved down to Louisiana I was working for a construction company and in order to get out to the temporary office at the construction site I would drive through a town called Ponchatoula. One day as I was driving through it, I heard God say in my heart to stop in a church that I was passing. It looked like a nice enough church from the outside, but I wasn't quite sure it was God so I didn't stop. However, I wasn't being obedient so God continued to speak to me about stopping at the church so one day I finally did. I didn't really know what to do since the only instruction I had was to go. So I walked into the church office and the secretary asked if she could help me. I said, "Well I am not sure, I felt like God told me to stop here, but I don't really know why." She asked if I would like to speak to the pastor and I said sure. Now I was thinking maybe the pastor has an encouraging word for me or something. But as the pastor walked up to me I felt like the Holy Spirit said this is an evil man. I was really taken aback and thought that I was just judging him. I tried to drown out the negativity I was feeling, which I later found really was the Holy Spirit. We talked for a little bit and I told him that God told me to stop by but I wasn't sure why. I explained I worked for a construction company and he said he was thinking about having something built so maybe that was why God had brought me in. We exchanged phone numbers and that was it. I left wondering what that was really all about.

About three months later I was shocked when I heard a news story on TV that there was a sting operation at the church in Ponchatoula because the pastor was abusing children and involved in cult activity. I was dumbfounded to say the least. I later learned that it was one of the secretaries that came clean about all of the wickedness that was transpiring. I don't know if it was the secretary that I spoke to or not and I have no way of knowing whether me stopping in had any influence at all. But the point of the story is that God is not mocked. He is aware of everything that goes on within the church and He is not only aware, but He is doing something about it. God knows everything that is happening in His church – God is not mocked and pastors and ministries will be removed for theft, adultery, and perversion.

Some people have left the church because of its imperfections, but there is no perfect church. Our job is to trust and support our churches and our pastors. It is God's job to defend His name and to ensure the faithfulness of His servants. You may have been hurt in the past by churches or pastors, but do not fall prey to the lies of the enemy that want to stop the unity and effectiveness of Christ's body. God cares much more than you do about the condition of his churches and the faithfulness of His pastors. So let God be God and you be you. Let God deal with His churches and pastors and you deal with your support and honor and trust of those who are stewards of your soul. *"The elders who rule well are to be considered worthy of double honor, especially those who work hard at preaching and teaching"* (I Timothy 5:17). (NASB)

My pastor is one of those elders who is worthy of double honor and he has said before that the local church is the hope of the world and it is so true. I remember after hurricane Katrina how many churches and Christian organizations came forward to provide aid and support. FEMA and the Red Cross helped and provided much needed support, but the local church did indeed rise and shine. Two days after the storm I was at Healing Place church in Baton Rouge, and because they were not badly hit by the storm they were having a supply and fundraising drive for victims. They had shelters set up for those who had to evacuate their homes, and people were coming by the hundreds to drop off food and supplies to the church so they could be distributed to storm victims. A couple of days later I went to volunteer in Gulfport, MS where still no one had power or any access to food because all of the stores were still shut down. There was a mission organization that set up base at one of the local strip malls and they had a drive through distribution center where cars would pull up and be given much needed supplies. People came from all over the country to bring supplies to the people in need. Now I'm sure not all of them were from churches but about 90% of them were. They came from Michigan and Ohio and California and Alabama and everywhere. Some came to help while others brought supplies. It was so amazing and encouraging to see the church in its finest hour. When there was no where else to turn and no one else to help – it was the church – the body of Christ that came to the rescue. The local church truly is the hope of the world because it is the tangible hand of Jesus helping hurting people.

The church is a house of prayer, not a religious club or marketing and fundraising business. The church is a place to come and meet with the living God, not to just see pictures and paintings of Him. The church is a place to come and confess your sins and be healed and set free, not a place of guilt and condemnation. The church is a place where every nation, tribe and tongue gather together, not a place of segregation and prejudice. The church is a place to worship God from your heart and not a place to be pretentious or play dress up. The church is a life altering place of surrender, not a social club that you go to twice a week for status. The church is a place where all are welcome and equal in the eyes of God, not a place for the elite to show favoritism. The church is a lifestyle that you live and breathe every day of your life, not a vacation spot where you visit a couple of times a year. The church is a place to proclaim the Good News to people and not beat them up or tear them down. The church is a place where the Word of God is proclaimed in truth and purity and not watered down to avoid offending. The Church is a place where the Kingdom of God expands, the Word of God is preached, the light exposes darkness and the name of Jesus is lifted high.

Lord, thank You for Your church where we as believers can be unified to fulfill Your purpose. Forgive us for the times we've been judgmental or critical and fought amongst ourselves. Help us to see others as You see them and to unite as one body with one purpose, to proclaim the message of Your Son. We praise You Lord, and give You thanks that the gates of Hell will not prevail against Your bride. Amen.

Complete & Reflect On Weekly Activity

THANKABILITY

Thank – to express gratitude or appreciation to.

Ability – power or capacity to do or act physically, mentally, legally morally or financially.

Thankability – the power or capacity to express gratitude or appreciation.

Unfortunately, it really is true that sometimes you don't know what you have until it's gone. That's why I am encouraging you not to let what you have slip away. Don't wait another day to say thanks and to appreciate whatever it is that you have no matter how small or insignificant it may be in the world's eyes. Don't wait until you're laid off to be thankful for your job. Don't wait until your marriage is on the rocks to be thankful for your spouse. Don't wait until your kids have left the house to appreciate them. Don't wait until your possessions rust and decay before you're thankful for them. Seize the moment! Change your attitude! Take every opportunity to be thankful for what you have. Choose to be thankful today!

Thanksgiving is worship when it is directed toward God. Even when we say thank you to others, if we realize that what they are providing is really coming from the hand of God, then in our hearts we can be thanking and praising God. I know that many people may be going through tough times. Just today my wife and I had a heated discussion (our kids call them arguments, but that doesn' t sound as sanctified) about what we were going to do this summer with our finances and about her finding a job or me finding a second job. Our checking account is overdrawn and I don' t know what the answer is. But I do know this - I thanked God today for everything that we do have, even for the food in our cupboards, the gas in our cars and the jobs that we currently have that continue to provide us income, and I' m believing that He' ll multiply it. God is so faithful and so gracious and we have seen Him come through time and time again as we have been at the end of our rope with nowhere to turn. Turn to Him today and trust in Him and in His provision, even if it looks different from what you planned.

In these times and in this generation, we especially need to know what it means to be content and grateful. It has been said that we are living in the first generation that as a whole can' t expect to do financially better than their parents. That probably has something to do with the fact that my mom and dad' s generation saw their parents go through the Great Depression and they were just thankful to have jobs and stayed in them for 30 years. These days we have recruiters, head hunters and temp agencies because people change jobs and careers like our parents changed underwear! Part of that probably has to do with our search for significance and our desire to do better, and part of it probably has to do with not being content with what we have and not knowing what it looks like to have financial hardship. I know there are a lot of legitimate reasons to change jobs and I have had more than my share, but that doesn' t change the goal of being content with what we have. Something is not always better on the other side. The grass is not always greener somewhere else. We may need to open our eyes and see the green where we are at.

The other thing that I want to communicate as we conclude our study of how to have the ability to be thankful in everything at all times, is how important it is to influence our greater communities and countries to return to being thankful toward God. Two of the best books I've read recently are Gary Smalley's book <u>Your Relationship With God</u> and Brother Yun's book <u>The Heavenly Man</u>. In both of these books these great men of God share stories about losing their focus and their orientation toward God. They both have experiences in which they warn of getting caught up in the world and losing their perspective about their original relationship with God. *"I have this against you that you have left your first love"* (Rev. 2:4).^(NASB) They both warn of this in their books. We must return to our first love in this country and globally as well.

At some point in time we have lost our first love and the relationship we had with God as a people and a country. We have become lukewarm saying *"I am rich, I have become wealthy, and have need of nothing"* (Rev. 3:17a). ^(NASB) It's easy to see how we've taken God for granted. A hundred years ago we needed God to grow our crops and we prayed for rain. Of course there was prayer in school – we needed Him to bless our crops. It's much harder to see the connection now that we just need a computer or electronic gadget. But God is still God. He hasn't moved. He's still on His throne and every good and perfect gift is still from Him. Hopefully, we will return to Him and give Him the thanks and praise He deserves and always has. Somewhere along the way our thanks and praise stopped, but His blessings kept on coming. We have been reaping the rewards of our ancestors and their relationship with God.

Now is the time to return to Him and enjoy the relationship that He designed us to have and the rewards that follow. *"...Therefore be zealous and repent. Behold, I stand at the door and knock. If anyone hears My voice and opens the door, I will come in to him and dine with him, and he with Me. To him who overcomes I will grant to sit with Me on My throne, as I also overcame and sat down with My Father on His throne"* (Revelation 3:19b-21). (NASB) But our country will not turn on its own. We have strayed so far but God is able to restore the years that the locusts have eaten. But again our country will not turn on its own. We must fulfill the Great Commission by reaching people and building their lives into mature disciples. Prayer isn't going to just be back in schools, abortion will not just end, gay marriage will not just disappear and evolution will not just fade from the text books. We must diligently seek God, return to Him, give Him thanks and praise, ask Him for strategies and fight for what God gave us – a Nation UNDER God. God wants us to vote, He wants us to promote His agenda and to return to His ways. And we must do it all in love and let Him win the battles. Our fight is not against flesh and blood. We must speak the truth in love and pray for God to return His favor to our country.

Be thankful with whatever circumstances you are in or wherever you may be in life. Maybe you're in the fight of your life with your health. Maybe the chaos is too much between home, work, finances, kids and everything else being thrown at you. Maybe your relationships seem to be falling apart. Maybe you're starting over at age 42 or maybe you're facing a pay cut or increased pressure or work load. Maybe you're working harder for less money than you ever have in your life. Maybe you had different plans. Maybe it would have been better if you would have done it differently. You may not understand but, be thankful for what you have and for where you are. It could always be worse and there are plenty of people who would love to be in the position you're in, if not in this country than certainly in another country. So no matter how difficult your circumstances may be or how unplanned, unfair or unexpected, take time to gain a new perspective and thank God for the blessings you do have. Focus on that instead of what you don' t have. Look at the two fish and the five loaves and give thanks for them. Don' t look at the thousands of obstacles that come to try and steal your joy and gratefulness.

Make a decision that for the rest of your days, no matter what your circumstances are, that you will give thanks for whatever you have no matter where you are and how small the blessing. There is something supernatural about giving thanks to God for what you have – when Jesus broke the bread and gave thanks it multiplied and He fed the thousands. After walking on the road to Emmaus with men that didn' t recognize Him, Jesus broke bread with them and gave thanks and their eyes were opened. So believe today for revelation and supernatural provision as you give thanks to God. Believe for God to supernaturally show up in your circumstances in His way and in His timing, and while you wait, maintain the posture of thankability – being thankful in everything at all times.

BIBLIOGRAPHY

Dayton, Howard. *Your Money Counts*, Cumming, GA: Crown Financial Ministries, 1996.

Kendrick, Stephen & Alex. *The Love Dare,* Nashville, TN: B&H Publishing Group, 2008.

Shook, Kerry & Chris. *One Month To Live*. Colorado Springs, CO: WaterBrook Press, 2008.

Smalley, Gary. *Your Relationship With God,* Colorado Springs, CO: Tyndale House, 2006.

Wilkinson, Bruce. *Beyond Jabez*. Sisters, Oregon: Multnomah Publishers, 2005.

Yun, Brother. *The Heavenly Man*. Grand Rapids, MI: Kreegal Publications, 2002.

THANKABILITY LIST

_____

_____

_____

_____

_____

_____

_____

_____

_____

_____

_____

_____

_____

_____

_____

_____

_____

_____

_____

_____

_____

_____

_____

_____

_____

THANKABILITY LIST

_____

_____

_____

_____

_____

_____

_____

_____

_____

_____

_____

_____

_____

_____

_____

_____

_____

_____

_____

_____

_____

_____

_____

_____

_____

THANKABILITY LIST

_____
_____
_____
_____
_____
_____
_____
_____
_____
_____
_____
_____
_____
_____
_____
_____
_____
_____
_____
_____
_____
_____
_____
_____

THANKABILITY JOURNAL

_____
_____
_____
_____
_____
_____
_____
_____
_____
_____
_____
_____
_____
_____
_____
_____
_____
_____
_____
_____
_____
_____
_____
_____
_____
_____

THANKABILITY JOURNAL

_____
_____
_____
_____
_____
_____
_____
_____
_____
_____
_____
_____
_____
_____
_____
_____
_____
_____
_____
_____
_____
_____
_____
_____
_____

THANKABILITY JOURNAL

THANKABILITY JOURNAL

_____

_____

_____

_____

_____

_____

_____

_____

_____

_____

_____

_____

_____

_____

_____

_____

_____

_____

_____

_____

_____

_____

_____

_____

_____

_____

_____

_____

THANKABILITY JOURNAL

THANKABILITY JOURNAL

THANKABILITY NOTES

_____

_____

_____

_____

_____

_____

_____

_____

_____

_____

_____

_____

_____

_____

_____

_____

_____

_____

_____

_____

_____

_____

_____

_____

_____

THANKABILITY NOTES

THANKABILITY NOTES

THANKABILITY NOTES

4846814R0

Made in the USA
Charleston, SC
24 March 2010